# This Book Is a Co...
# Study Guide to the Online Course.

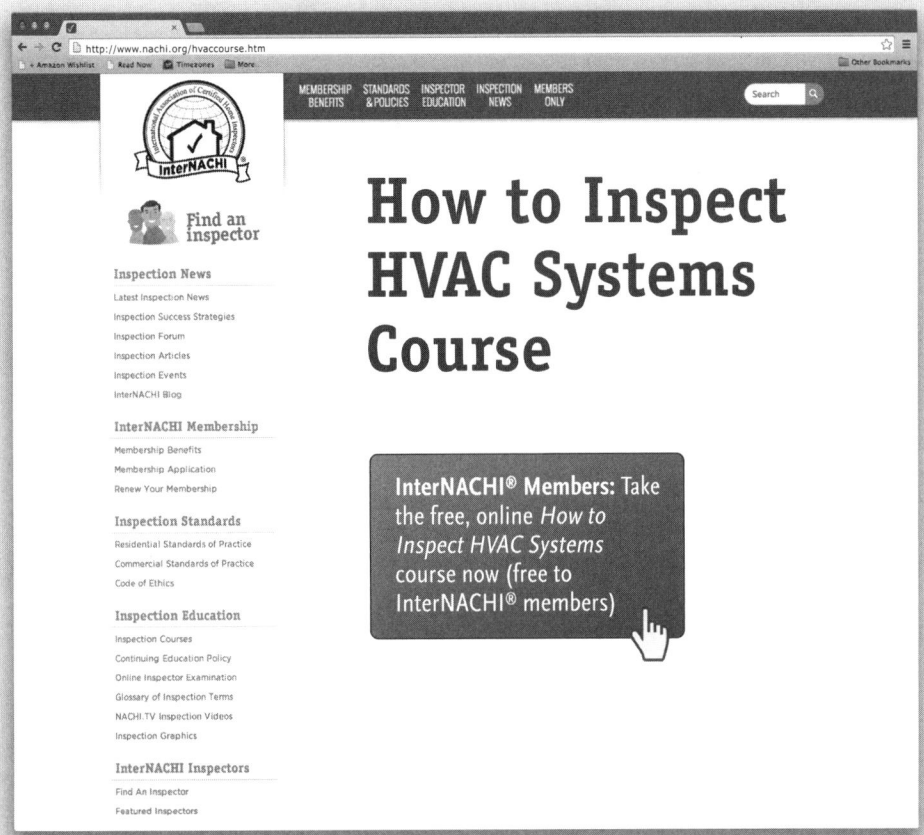

# The course is free for all InterNACHI® members.

**Upon successfully completing the online course and passing the final exam, you will receive a Certificate of Completion and be able to:**

· inspect the heating system and related components;

· inspect the cooling system and related components;

· inspect the fireplace, solid-fuel burning appliances, and chimneys;

· identify and describe each system and related component of the heating, cooling and fireplace systems; and

· describe any defects you observed at the heating, cooling and fireplace systems.

Take the online course at **www.nachi.org/hvaccourse**

# Inspecting HVAC Systems

The purpose of this publication is to provide accurate and useful information for home inspectors in order to perform an inspection of the heating, ventilation, and air-conditioning (HVAC) system at a residential property. This manual covers the components of common residential HVAC systems, including: warm-air, hydronic, steam and electric heating systems; air-conditioning systems; and heat-pump systems. This guide also refers to the InterNACHI® Residential Standards of Practice with regard to recommended inspection protocols. For more information, visit www.NACHI.org.

## To order additional training books, visit www.InspectorOutlet.com

### Authors:

Ben Gromicko and Nick Gromicko

### Graphics:

Lisaira Vega, Levi Nelson, Erica Saurey, Cherise Peterson & Chris Krowiak

### Editor:

Kate Tarasenko / Crimea River, LLC

### Layout & Design:

Jessica Langer

## www.NACHI.org

# Table of Contents

# Introduction

## Learning Objectives

The inspector will demonstrate a practical understanding and comprehension of this material by reading and studying the sections, taking the practice quizzes at the end of selected sections, and taking the online course in its entirety and successfully passing a timed online exam. After successful completion of the online course, the student will be able to perform an inspection of the HVAC system at a residential property, according to the InterNACHI® Standards of Practice for Performing a General Home Inspection.

This guide lists the particular section of the InterNACHI® Residential Standards of Practice pertaining to HVAC inspections. The full text of the Standards can be found online at **www.nachi.org/sop**

# Inspection Tools

There are many tools that can be used for inspecting an HVAC system during residential and commercial property inspections.

## Flashlight

A flashlight is handy for inspecting the HVAC system. The outdoor condenser unit may be in dark shade, under dense vegetation, or under a structural covering, such as a deck or balcony. Inside the house, the HVAC system may be located in an attic, crawlspace, or dark basement. The inspection of the internal components of the system may require illumination for some instances, including:

- looking at the ribbon burners inside the combustion chamber;
- looking at the interior of the combustion chamber through a viewing portal; or
- looking at the air-filtering system that is installed inside the ductwork.

## Moisture Meter

A moisture meter is used to detect and confirm moisture. It could be used to confirm water and condensation problems, and to confirm that a building material is saturated with water. High-efficiency condensing HVAC systems produce excessive condensate, and that water needs to be controlled and discharged. Oftentimes, there are condensate lines or sweating suction lines that leak onto building materials. Those leaks might be confirmed with the use of a moisture meter. There are meters that are non-invasive and meters that have invasive probes. Learn how to inspect for moisture during a property inspection at **www.nachi.org/moisturecourse.htm**

## Infrared Camera

You should be professionally trained and certified to use an infrared camera. Thermography is an effective means of inspecting for water leaks and moisture problems. For an introductory course on infrared thermography, please visit **www.nachi.org/infrared-thermography-inspection-training-video-course**

## Tape Measure

A tape measure can be used to measure the slope of a flue connector pipe, the height of a chimney stack above the roof surface, and the clearance around the outdoor condenser unit from other structures.

## Screwdriver, Awl or Probe

An awl or probe of some kind can be used to check for wood rot and damage caused by a leak from a condensing unit. A screwdriver may be needed to remove an access panel or cover at the HVAC system.

## Binoculars

Binoculars can be used to look where physical, up-close access is restricted. If an air conditioner is installed inside an attic, the water-leak catch pan typically has a drainpipe discharge at the eaves area. This drainpipe may not be readily visible from the ground without binoculars.

## Ladder

A ladder can be used to gain access to those high areas that are not readily accessible or visible from ground level.

## Magnet

A magnet can be used to tell the difference between aluminum pipes and steel pipes, and galvanized steel flashing from copper flashing.

## Coveralls

Coveralls or overalls protect your clothes. These are handy when moving through a crawlspace and for inspecting under a low deck or porch.

## Booties

You can put on some shoe booties prior to entering the house you're inspecting. Booties protect the floors. This demonstrates care and consideration for your client's property.

## Gloves

Protect yourself. Use personal protection equipment (PPE), including a simple pair of gloves. Gloves will protect your hands from insect bites, scratches from vegetation, dirt and soil, debris, splinters, and cuts from sharp edges of the HVAC components.

## Kneepads

It is important to protect your knees while crawling around, particularly when the ground surface is rough and covered with rocks and stones. Kneepads are handy when kneeling in front of the HVAC system and conducting your inspection.

# Inspection Procedures

Many inspectors start their home inspection by evaluating the exterior first. The exterior inspection may include parts of the HVAC system. For example, a home that has a fuel-fired heating system requires venting of its combustion gases and byproducts to the outside. The chimney stack or flue exhaust pipes will need to be inspected. While you are conducting your roof inspection, you'll need to check the chimney and/or flue pipes that penetrate or come in contact with the roof system. When inspecting the exterior grounds, you may stop at the condenser unit outside and shift gears from inspecting the exterior to inspecting the HVAC system. It is up to the inspector to choose the path to take when inspecting the systems of the house. Do you inspect the exterior components of the HVAC system while you are inspecting the exterior of the house?

## Step Back

Figure out the various components of the house by stepping back. Identify the location of some of the systems, such as the electrical service, HVAC unit, chimney structures, plumbing entrance, landscaping features, property boundaries, shared utilities or components, inspection restrictions, and other features and systems.

## Move Closer

Next, move closer to the house to get a better look. Many inspectors follow the front walk or driveway that leads to the house as they approach. You may choose a clockwise direction to move around the perimeter of the house. In this close-up inspection of the exterior, you are looking for details of the HVAC system. Is there an air-conditioning unit? Are there window or through-wall air-conditioner units? If there's a chimney, is the heating system connected to it? Where does the air conditioner's condensate discharge? Get behind vegetation, and look under, crawl under, reach up, look into, and touch, measure and probe.

## Time

The exterior, including the roof system and exterior HVAC components, may take up to a third of the total time of the home inspection.

## Destroyer

Water (or moisture) is one of the main concerns when inspecting the HVAC system. Think about water; it is the greatest destroyer of houses. Look for breaches and holes in the siding where the exterior HVAC components are located. If the system is producing condensate, figure out where it goes and how it's being managed. For example, a suction line of an operating air-conditioning system that is not insulated properly may produce excessive condensate and humidity, under certain conditions. Pay attention to excessive humidity levels that may be produced by a maladjusted component.

# InterNACHI® SOP

This section covers specific items in InterNACHI's Home Inspection Standards of Practice and how they relate to the items and conditions an inspector may observe while inspecting the HVAC system at a residential property. At the end of this section, you should be able to:

- list at least four things an inspector is required to inspect; and
- list at least four things an inspector is not required to inspect.

## InterNACHI's Home Inspection Standards of Practice

The following are excerpts from the Standards of Practice as they pertain to inspecting the heating, ventilation and cooling (HVAC) system at a residential property. The full text of the Standards can be found online at **www.nachi.org/sop.htm**

### 1. Definitions and Scope

**1.1.** A **general home inspection** is a non-invasive, visual examination of the accessible areas of a residential property (as delineated below), performed for a fee, which is designed to identify defects within specific systems and components defined by these Standards that are both observed and deemed material by the inspector. The scope of work may be modified by the Client and Inspector prior to the inspection process.

    I. The general home inspection is based on the observations made on the date of the inspection, and not a prediction of future conditions.

    II. The general home inspection will not reveal every issue that exists or ever could exist, but only those material defects observed on the date of the inspection.

**1.2.** A **material defect** is a specific issue with a system or component of a residential property that may have a significant, adverse impact on the value of the property, or that poses an unreasonable risk to people. The fact that a system or component is near, at, or beyond the end of its normal, useful life is not, in itself, a material defect.

**1.3.** A **general home inspection report** shall identify, in written format, defects within specific systems and components defined by these Standards that are both observed and deemed material by the inspector. Inspection reports may include additional comments and recommendations.

[...]

### 3.4. Heating

    I. The inspector shall inspect:

        A. the heating system, using normal operating controls.

    II. The inspector shall describe:

        A. the location of the thermostat for the heating system;

        B. the energy source; and

        C. the heating method.

    III. The inspector shall report as in need of correction:

        A. any heating system that did not operate; and

B. if the heating system was deemed inaccessible.

IV. The inspector is not required to:

A. inspect or evaluate the interior of flues or chimneys, fire chambers, heat exchangers, combustion air systems, fresh-air intakes, makeup air, humidifiers, dehumidifiers, electronic air filters, geothermal systems, or solar heating systems.

B. inspect fuel tanks or underground or concealed fuel supply systems.

C. determine the uniformity, temperature, flow, balance, distribution, size, capacity, BTU, or supply adequacy of the heating system.

D. light or ignite pilot flames.

E. activate heating, heat pump systems, or other heating systems when ambient temperatures or other circumstances are not conducive to safe operation or may damage the equipment.

F. override electronic thermostats.

G. evaluate fuel quality.

H. verify thermostat calibration, heat anticipation, or automatic setbacks, timers, programs or clocks.

I. measure or calculate the air for combution, ventilation, or dilution of flue gases for appliances.

## 3.5. Cooling

I. The inspector shall inspect:

A. the cooling system, using normal operating controls.

II. The inspector shall describe:

A. the location of the thermostat for the cooling system; and

B. if the cooling method was deemed accessible.

III. The inspector shall report as in need of correction:

A. any cooling system that did not operate; and

B. if the cooling system was deemed inaccessible.

IV. The inspector is not required to:

A. determine the uniformity, temperature, flow, balance, distribution, size, capacity, BTU, or supply adequacy of the cooling system.

B. inspect portable window units, through-wall units, or electronic air filters.

C. operate equipment or systems if the exterior temperature is below 65° Fahrenheit, or when other circumstances are not conducive to safe operation or may damage the equipment.

D. inspect or determine thermostat calibration, cooling anticipation, or automatic setbacks or clocks.

E. examine electrical current, coolant fluids or gases, or coolant leakage.

## Comments on the SOP

Home inspectors are not HVAC technicians or experts. We are not indoor air quality experts. We are property inspectors performing property inspections according to an established standard. We are substantially complying with the InterNACHI® Residential Standards of Practice. We are employing the best non-invasive, visual-only inspection techniques to perform the inspection of the HVAC system.

The inspection is not technically exhaustive. That means that the inspection is not a comprehensive and detailed examination beyond the scope of a property inspection that would involve or include, but would not be limited to: dismantling, specialized knowledge or training, special equipment, measurements, calculations, testing, research, analysis, or other means.

Consider communicating to your client that there may be problems with the property that exist during the inspection that will not be found or discovered because they are beyond the scope of the home inspection.

We **inspect** the heating and cooling systems that are permanently installed at the property. This means that we have to visually observe readily accessible systems and components safely, using normal operating controls, and opening readily accessible panels and areas in accordance with the Standards of Practice. Something is accessible if it can be approached or entered by the inspector safely, without difficulty, fear or danger.

A **component** is a permanently installed or attached fixture, element or part of a system. The blower fan of a forced warm-air furnace is one example of a component of the heating system.

We can **activate** a component. Activating means to turn on, supply power to, or enable systems, equipment or devices to become active using only normal operating controls. An example of this is turning on only the blower fan using the thermostat control.

The **condition** of a component is its visible and conspicuous state of being. An inspector can report on the component's condition as being functional. A component can be functional, or performing, or able to perform a function. A physically damaged blower fan is a component in a condition that is not functional.

In the **inspection report**, we can describe, in written format, a system or component by its type or other observed characteristics in order to distinguish it from other components used for the same purpose.

An inspector is required to describe and identify, in written format, **material defects** observed. A material defect is a condition of a residential property, or any portion of it, that would have a significant, adverse impact on the value of the property, or that involves an unreasonable risk to people on the property.

The inspector shall inspect the heating systems using **normal operating controls**. There are a few controls on a typical heating system, including the thermostat and service shut-off switch.

We should be able to describe the **energy source**. The heating system may use a variety of fuels, including electricity. We should describe the **heating method**. There are several ways a heating system can distribute heat energy to the rooms and spaces of a building. Inspectors need to inspect and be able to describe, in writing, how the system supplies heat to the building. One example may be that the heating system is described as having No. 2 fuel oil as the energy source, and the system is a forced warm-air heating system that uses a blower fan to distribute air through the ducts or pipes.

Termination Clearances of Mechanical Draft and Direct-Vent Venting Systems

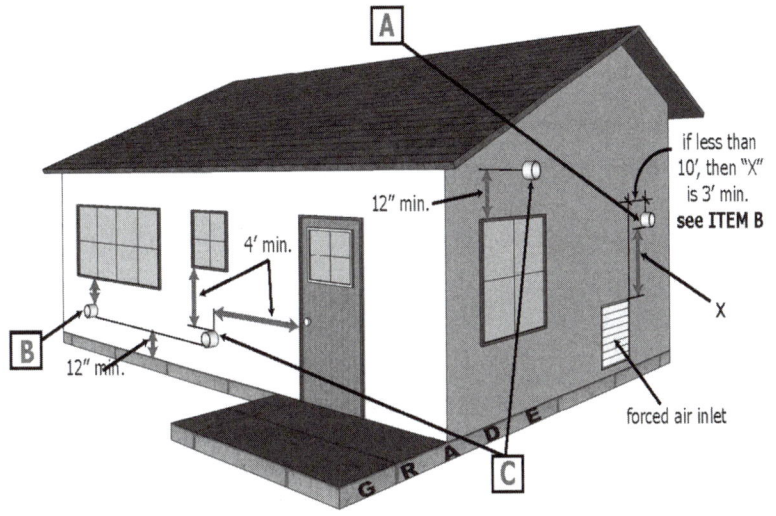

if less than 10', then "X" is 3' min.
see ITEM B

12" min.

4' min.

12" min.

X

forced air inlet

GRADE

**ITEM A:** A mechanical draft-venting system shall terminate at least 3 feet above any forced-air inlet located within 10 feet.

**ITEM B:** The vent termination of a direct-vent appliance with an input of 10,000 BTU/hr or less must be located at least 6 inches away from any air opening into the building. If the input is over 10,000 BTU/hr but not over 50,000 BTU/hr, the vent termination must be located at least 9 inches away from any air opening. If the input is over 50,000 BTU/hr, the vent termination must be located at least 9 inches away from any air opening. The bottom of the vent termination and air intake must be at least 1 foot above grade.

**ITEM C:** The vent, excluding direct-vent appliances, shall terminate at least 4 feet below, 4 feet horizontally from, or 1 foot above any door, operable window, or gravity air inlet into any building. The bottom of the vent termination shall be located at least 1 foot above grade.

You are required to inspect the central cooling equipment using normal operating controls, which include the thermostat and service shut-off switches. A portable window or through-wall air-conditioning unit is not considered a central cooling system. You do not have to inspect a window, through-wall or portable air conditioner unless it is permanently installed and hard-wired into the electrical system, or unless your state's SOP requires that you do.

We are not required to use a ladder to inspect a house. Many inspectors use binoculars to get a better look at components that are above their heads. When moving around the house, look up and inspect the eaves, soffits and fascia components. If a heating or cooling system is installed in an attic space and the unit is producing condensate, you will find a condensate drain line coming from the eaves and discharging to the exterior. That small pipe may be difficult to see from the ground without the use of binoculars.

If a heating or cooling system does not turn on or does not operate, the inspector should note this in the inspection report. We are not required to ignite a pilot flame or turn on a system that has been turned off. If you believe that activating an HVAC system may actually cause damage to the system, you are not required to turn it on. For example, the Standards specifically state that if the temperature is below 65° F, or when other circumstances are not conducive to the safe operation of the cooling system, you are not required to activate and inspect the cooling system.

If the heating or cooling system is deemed to be inaccessible, the inspector should report it as such. There may be a condenser unit located on top of a flat roof. If that roof is inaccessible to the inspector, then so is the condenser unit. The inspector should report how or why the particular system or component of a system was not accessible.

Inspection reports may include **recommendations** regarding conditions reported, or recommendations for correction, monitoring, or further evaluation by the appropriate professionals, but this is not required.

We are not required to inspect the interior of flues or chimneys, fire chambers, heat exchangers or combustion-air systems. Most of the internal components of a heating system are beyond the scope of a home inspection.

Humidifiers and dehumidifiers are beyond the scope of a home inspection. We are not required to inspect them. Problems that are found at the heating system are sometimes caused by a failure at the humidifier. Humidifiers involve a lot of moisture, water and condensate. If the humidifier is malfunctioning, it could have a deleterious impact on the heating system.

Geothermal and solar heating systems are not part of a home inspection, according to the Standards.

BURIED OIL STORAGE TANK

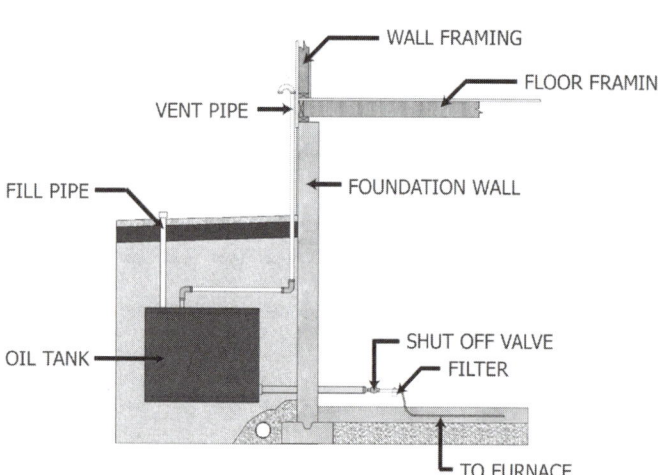

You do not have to inspect the fuel storage tank if it is buried underground, but you are required to describe any visible fuel storage systems.

Inspectors do not have to determine the balance of the system, its BTU capacity, its size, or its ability to adequately supply heated or cooled air to the building. You are not required to determine the size, BTU or tonnage of the air-conditioning system, according to the InterNACHI® Standards of Practice.

If the heating system is a boiler, the inspector should verify the presence or absence of temperature/pressure-relief valves and/or Watts 210 valves. You are not required to test, operate, open or close safety controls, manual stop valves, and/or temperature or pressure-relief valves.

At hydronic heating systems, you do not have to inspect water storage tanks, pressure pumps, or bladder tanks. On boiler systems, you do not have to determine the effectiveness of anti-siphon or back-flow prevention devices.

Electronic air filters can be dangerous to inspect if they are not safely wired or properly installed. You are not required to inspect electronic air-filtering devices.

A general home inspection does not include outbuildings. If there is a heating or cooling system in an outbuilding, many inspectors will note the existence of the system and that the additional structure, which includes the HVAC system, is beyond the scope of the inspection. Many inspectors charge an additional fee to inspect outbuildings.

In summary, an inspector should be able to inspect and describe the heating and cooling systems. An inspection report shall describe and identify, in written format, the inspected heating and cooling systems and components of the dwelling, and the material defects observed. Inspection reports may include recommendations for the correction, monitoring, and/or further evaluation by professionals of conditions reported, but this is not required by InterNACHI's SOP.

# Quiz #1

1. T/F: A home inspection is a non-invasive, visual examination of a residential dwelling.

☑ True

☐ False

2. T/F: A home inspector is required to describe the energy source.

☑ True

☐ False

3. T/F: A home inspector is not required to describe the heating method.

☐ True

☑ False

4. T/F: The inspector is required to inspect window and through-wall air-conditioning units.

☐ True

☑ False

**Answer Key is on page 117.**

# Introduction to HVAC

This training manual covers the principles of heating, ventilating and air conditioning (HVAC) for residential and commercial property inspectors. Heating, ventilation and air conditioning are each used in an attempt to control the environment within an enclosure, whether it is a room, space, or a dwelling.

People have been trying to control indoor heat and ventilation since prehistoric times. Over the centuries, the technology of heating has advanced from simple efforts to keep the body warm to very sophisticated systems. Ventilation has been used for a very long time as well, dating back to the days when royalty was cooled by servants and slaves fanning them using large palm fronds and feathers.

Ventilation became important during the Industrial Revolution in order to protect workers and increase their productivity, as well as the efficiency of machinery.

Air conditioning is a relatively recent development and involves the control of temperature, humidity, and air cleanliness.

It wasn't until after 1945 that the use of air conditioning or simple cooling of the air became widespread. Modern air-conditioning systems have greatly evolved from the times of simply hanging wet towels across an open window.

Today, air-conditioning systems do not simply cool the air, but they actually condition it by controlling the air's temperature, moisture content, movement and cleanliness.

Understanding the basics of heating, ventilation and air conditioning is essential for a property inspector.

# Heat Fundamentals

There are essentially three ways that heat moves from one area to another. When bodies of unequal temperatures are near each other, heat leaves one body and goes to the other. Heat moves from the hotter body, and the colder body absorbs it. The greater the difference in temperature, the greater the rate of flow of the heat.

Heat moves from one body to another by the following ways:

- radiation;
- conduction; and
- convection.

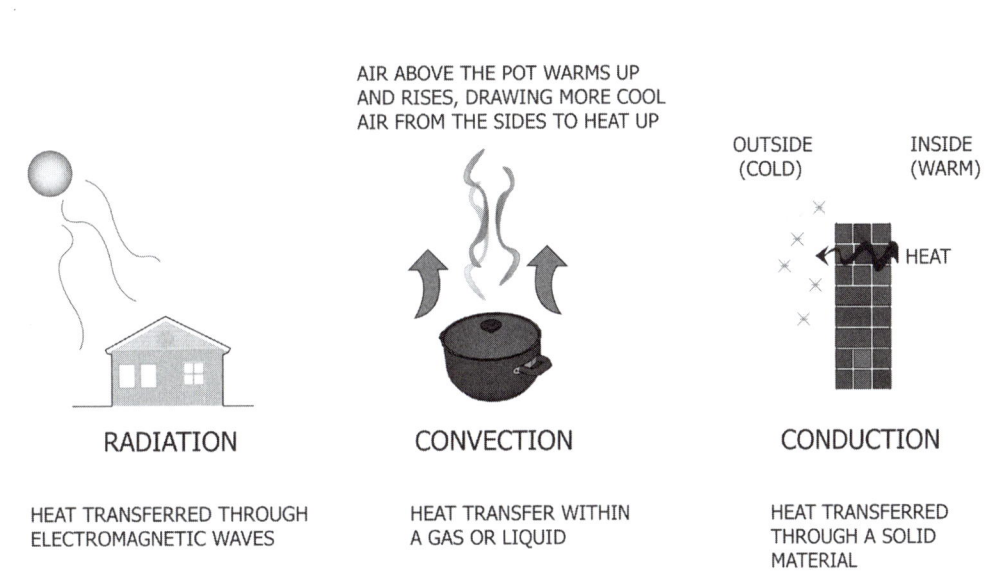

HEAT TRANSFER METHODS

AIR ABOVE THE POT WARMS UP
AND RISES, DRAWING MORE COOL
AIR FROM THE SIDES TO HEAT UP

OUTSIDE (COLD)     INSIDE (WARM)

HEAT

RADIATION

HEAT TRANSFERRED THROUGH
ELECTROMAGNETIC WAVES

CONVECTION

HEAT TRANSFER WITHIN
A GAS OR LIQUID

CONDUCTION

HEAT TRANSFERRED
THROUGH A SOLID
MATERIAL

Radiation is the transfer of heat energy by electromagnetic wave motion. Heat is transferred in direct rays. It travels in a straight line from the source to the body. The closer you are to a hot object, the warmer you feel. The intensity of the heat radiated from the object decreases as the distance from the object increases.

You feel cool in a room that has a cold floor, walls and ceiling. The amount of heat loss from your body in that room depends on the relative temperature of the objects in that room. The colder the floor is (relative to the temperature of your feet), the greater the heat loss will be from your body by just standing there. If the floor, walls and ceiling of that room are relatively warmer than your body temperature, then heat will be radiated to your body from those objects and surfaces.

Radiant heating in residential buildings includes piping and electrical wiring in floors, walls and ceilings. Radiant heat emits in all directions. Reflective materials are commonly used in a radiant heat-emitting system in order to direct and control where the heat is emitted.

Conduction is the transfer of heat from one molecule to another, or through one substance to another. It is heat that moves from one body to another by direct contact. For example, heat is transferred by conduction from a hot boiler heat exchanger to the cooler water passing through it. When you touch a suction line of an air conditioner and it feels cool, that's heat energy moving from your warm hand to the cooler copper tube via conduction.

Convection is known by most people from the phrase "heat rises." Convection is the transfer of heat by warming the air next to a hot surface, and then moving that warm air. It's the transfer of heat by the motion of the heated matter itself. The air moves from one place to another, carrying heat along with it. Since warm air is lighter than the cool air around it, the warm air (or heat) rises.

Warm fluids tend to rise while the surrounding cool fluids fall. This rising-and-falling action forms loops — convective loops — by which warm air rises and cool air falls. Early warm-air gravity furnaces used the principles of convective loops. In a gravity system, the warm air rises and the cool air falls, and this is how the gravity warm-air heating system circulates air.

Forced-air furnaces function primarily by convection. Heat is transferred to the air, and the air is circulated throughout the house. Systems that heat water and use radiators and baseboards as their heat-emitting devices operate via convection and, to a lesser extent, radiation.

A radiator needs air to be moving freely around it in order to work effectively. A cover on a radiator may reduce the air flow around and through the radiator unit.

# Quiz #2

1. T/F: In two bodies of unequal temperatures, heat moves from the warmer body, and the colder body absorbs it.

☑ True
☐ False

2. Heat can move from one body to another by _____.

☐ ionization
☑ radiation
☐ capacitation

3. Forced-air furnaces function primarily by _____.

☑ convection
☐ radiation
☐ conduction

**Answer Key is on page 117.**

# Identify and Describe Heating Systems

## Four Furnace Categories

The 2018 International Fuel Gas Code (IFGC) puts furnaces in four categories based on flue vent pressures, flue gas temperatures (related to condensing or non-condensing), and vent pipe materials, as shown in Table 1.

|  | **Flue Negative Pressure** | **Flue Positive Pressure** |
|---|---|---|
| **Non-Condensing** | **Category I Vented Appliance**<br><br>An appliance that operates with a nonpositive vent static pressure and with a vent gas temperature that avoids excessive condensate production in the vent | **Category III Vented Appliance**<br><br>An appliance that operates with a positive vent static pressure and with a vent gas temperature that avoids excessive condensate production in the vents. |
| **Condensing** | *Not common in residental*<br>**Category II Vented Appliance**<br><br>An appliance that operates with a nonpositive vent static pressure and with a vent gas temperature that can cause excessive condensate production in the vent. | *Common for Home*<br>**Category IV Vented Appliance**<br><br>An appliance that operates with a positive vent static pressure and with a vent gas temperature that can cause excessive condensate production in the vent. |

Table 1. The International Fuel Gas Code identifies four categories for combustion furnaces and water heaters based on combustion type (sealed or unsealed), vent pipe pressure, and vent pipe temperature.

Chapter 5 of the International Fuel Gas Code identifies four categories for combustion furnaces and water heaters based on combustion type (sealed or unsealed), vent pipe pressure, and vent pipe temperature.

A common vent flue pipe material for Category I is a Type B vent. For Category II, it depends on the manufacturer. Category III may be stainless steel. And a common pipe material for Category IV is PVC plastic. Type B vents are designed for venting non-condensing gas appliances equipped with a draft hood and fan-assisted appliances that operate with a non-positive vent pressure. A Type B vent must never be installed on a Category III or IV gas-fired appliance. Type B, BW and L vents are designed for natural draft applications only, and they must not be used for vents under positive pressure.

## Category I

A Category I furnace operates with the flue at negative pressure with respect to the combustion appliance zone or CAZ (the room in which the furnace is located), and whether the stack temperature is hot enough to avoid condensation in the vent. The burner draws its combustion air from the CAZ. The combustion chamber is also open to the CAZ (for example, if you are standing next to the furnace, you can peer in and see the burner and the flames).

Older Category I furnaces use an open draft hood that allows dilution air to enter the vent pipe and mix with the exhaust gases. A draft diverter at the base of the flue protects the flame from downdrafts coming down the chimney or flue. These older furnaces are not mechanically drafted but are called natural draft (or atmospheric draft) because they rely entirely on high flue temperatures (relative to outside temperatures) to draw exhaust gases up and out of the flue. Because so much of the heat goes up the chimney, natural draft furnaces have very low Annual Fuel Utilization Efficiency (AFUE) ratings, usually less than 72%.

A newer type of Category 1 furnace replaced the draft hood with a small fan, referred to as an induced-draft fan, which pulls air through the combustion chamber, although the furnace still relies on flue temperatures to lift the combustion gases up the flue stack. The induced-draft fan helps to prevent backdrafting on startup and assists in getting the draft started. Once the vent pipe gets up to temperature (+140° F) and a draft is established, the pressure inside the vent pipe becomes negative with respect to the CAZ. Depending on the model, the induced draft fan may turn off but will continue to spin due to airflow. Category 1 furnaces that incorporate an induced-draft fan typically have cleaner or more complete combustion than their older counterparts and therefore expel less pollutants into the air. The byproducts of an +80% furnace are $CO_2$, N, and $H_2O$. Category 1 induced-draft furnaces typically have efficiencies of 80% to 82%.

An induced-draft fan-equipped furnace is considered a mechanically drafted furnace, according to the International Mechanical Code (IMC). However, because it relies on negative flue pressure to carry away combustion byproducts, it can, like the naturally drafted furnace, have the potential to backdraft. Backdrafting (when combustion gases spill down into the CAZ rather than going out the flue) can occur if the CAZ becomes depressurized with respect to the flue. This could occur if multiple exhaust fans and the dryer or the fireplace are operating at the same time.

Never install a Category I furnace using the CAZ as the return-air plenum; duct the return plenum to return registers in other parts of the house. The return-air side of the forced-air furnace should have no communication with the CAZ at all. The blower in Category I furnaces is meant to move a high volume of air against a relatively high pressure, approximately 0.5 inches water column (IWC) static pressure or 125 Pascals. The pressure in the vent pipe in a gas forced-air Category I furnace when it is 30° F outdoors is about -4 Pascals (0.016 IWC). Because Category I furnaces have an open combustion chamber, the big blower fan can easily overcome the small induced-draft fan and backdraft the furnace, pulling carbon monoxide into the open return on the furnace, and distributing it throughout the house via the supply ducts.

## Category II

Category II applies to some commercial furnaces but not commonly for residential furnaces, except for some boilers and wall-vented water heaters. Category II units also operate under negative or neutral vent pressure. Condensation of flue gases could occur. The vent systems have special provisions.

## Category III

Most Category III furnaces are high-efficiency oil furnaces with gun-type burners that force the fuel oil through a nozzle that emits the oil in an atomizing spray that mixes well with air for a more efficient burn. These oil furnaces have an efficiency range of 82% to 88%.

Category III appliances could also be tankless water heaters that vent using stainless steel pipe material.

A Category III furnace has a vent pipe that is under positive pressure and the furnace is non-condensing, meaning its flue gases only go through one heat exchanger, then exit through the vent at temperatures above 140° F. These appliances could produce condensation, although the are not considered to be "condensing appliances."

A Category III appliance vents through the wall or roof and is forced draft, meaning it is equipped with a combustion fan that is located before the burner to push air through the combustion chamber and out of the vent. The fan is continually operating when the burner is firing so the vent stack pressure is always positive.

The vent system flue must be airtight. Category III furnaces vent their exhaust gases outside through a sealed pipe so they cannot be backdrafted. They are typically installed as sealed combustion/direct-vent appliances, meaning they draw their combustion air directly from outside. The pipe for the incoming air may be a separate pipe from the exhaust pipe, or it may be the outer circle of a concentric pipe-within-a-pipe, where the inner pipe is the exhaust vent. Although it is not recommended, Category III furnaces are sometimes installed as non-direct vent appliances, where the combustion air is drawn from the CAZ and enters the furnace through a port on the combustion chamber, while exhaust gases vent to the outside via the single vent pipe.

### Category IV    *Our Furnace*

Category IV furnaces are combustion appliances that have a vent pipe under positive pressure and flue gases under 140° F. The vent exhaust is so low-temperature because all Category IV appliances are equipped with a secondary heat exchanger, where heat is further extracted from the combustion air as the water vapor (a byproduct of combustion) cools and condenses into liquid water. This liquid is drained to the outside through a condensate drain. The condensate is highly acidic (pH ≤3), so local code may require that it be pretreated before disposing to the sewer. Because the combustion gases are directed through a secondary heat exchanger, more heat is extracted, enabling gas-fired Category IV furnaces to achieve efficiencies of >90% AFUE. Category IV oil-fired furnaces can achieve efficiencies of 95% AFUE. Category IV furnaces with two-stage motors for high and low capacity can achieve AFUEs greater than 94%.

Like Category III furnaces, Category IV furnaces are forced-draft, meaning they are equipped with a fan to pull air through the combustion chamber and push the byproducts of combustion out of the furnace through a vent pipe; the vent pipe is sealed so they cannot be backdrafted.

Category IV furnaces should be installed as sealed-combustion/direct-vent appliances, which means their combustion chamber is sealed off from the CAZ, and they draw their combustion air from outside via a second vent pipe that brings combustion air directly to the combustion chamber from outside the home. Because nearly all of the heat in the combustion gases is removed by the two heat exchangers, the vent pipe for Category IV furnaces can be made of PVC. Manufacturers do not recommend installing Category IV furnaces as non-direct vent furnaces that draw their combustion air from the compliance zone. Always install the second vent pipe to bring combustion air in from outside.

# Identify and Describe the Heating System

According to InterNACHI's Standards of Practice, a home inspector shall identify and describe, in written format, the inspected systems and components of the dwelling. In the following sections, we will learn that most heating systems can be identified and described in just four ways.

## Heating Systems

There are many different types of heating systems. Each has its own characteristics that can be noted by a property inspector to identify and describe the type of heating system being inspected.

Most heating systems can be described according to one or more of the following broad categories:

- the heat-conveying medium;
- the fuel used;
- the nature of the heat; and
- the efficiency and capacity of the system.

The heat-conveying medium is what carries the heat from the source to the enclosure being heated. The fuel used is a distinguishing characteristic of a heating system. Wood, coal, oil and gas are used to produce heat. Electricity may be considered a fuel, but it can also be the heat-conveying medium. The nature of the heat is also a distinguishing characteristic. For example, it could be steam, or heat produced by combustion. The efficiency and capacity of the heating system can be cited to distinguish one heating system from another.

These four categories alone are not enough for most inspectors to sufficiently identify and describe the type of heating system that they are inspecting. The use of these categories and terms may be confusing to the inspector's clients. Other distinguishing characteristics and details are needed in order to identify and describe different types of heating systems in a concise manner that is specific to the property, as well as easily understood. Let's take a look at how heating systems can be identified and described in more detail, according to heat-conveying mediums.

## Heat-Conveying Mediums

For most inspectors, describing the heat-conveying medium is one of the main ways to identify and describe different types of heating systems. There are four heat-conveying mediums that can carry heat. They are air, water, steam and electricity.

For example, if the heating system is a high-efficiency, gas-fired furnace, then the heat-conveying medium is air. The inspector would use the heat-conveying medium as part of the identification and description of the heating system. In this example, the description would be a warm-air heating system, or, even more accurately, a gas warm-air furnace.

## Four Types of Heating Systems

Taking the previously listed four common heat-conveying mediums into consideration, most heating systems can be identified and described by a property inspector using the following four terms:

- warm-air heating system;
- hydronic heating system;
- steam-heating system; and
- electric heating system.

Most heating systems can be described in these four ways. They can be accurately identified and described using these terms, which are based on the four heat-conveying mediums: air, water, steam and electricity. The classification of a heating system based on its heat-conveying medium is a convenient method for property inspectors to use because it includes the vast majority of heating systems that are manufactured and used today.

## Heating Fuels

An inspector should describe the energy source or the type of heating fuel in the inspection report.

This additional information is valuable to the inspector's client. Specifying the type of heating fuel being used by the heating system helps in defining and distinguishing the type of heating system being inspected.

There are several types of heating fuels that are used today by most heating systems, including:

- fuel oil (No. 2);
- natural gas;
- propane;
- coal;
- electricity;
- wood;
- kerosene; and
- pellets.

Stating the type of heating fuel used is essential to accurately identifying and describing the heating system.

# Quiz #3

1. T/F: You may be able to describe a heating system by its heat-conveying medium.

    ☑ True

    ☐ False

2. T/F: Steam is considered a heat-conveying medium.

    ☑ True

    ☐ False

3. Most heating systems can be categorized in _____ ways.

    ☐ two

    ☑ four

    ☐ six

4. T/F: "Hydronic" describes a type of heating system.

    ☑ True

    ☐ False

**Answer Key is on page 117.**

# Gas, Gas Meters and Gas Pipes

## Natural Gas

Natural gas has no color or odor, and it's not toxic. It is, however, highly combustible. It only smells because a scent has been added to it in order to help us identify gas leaks. Natural gas has a specific gravity of about 0.6. Air has a specific gravity of 1. Natural gas is lighter than air. Propane has a specific gravity of 1.5. A propane leak tends to pool on the floor, which creates a dangerous situation.

To ignite natural gas, you need a mixture of gas and air that is conducive to ignition. If you have too little air in the mix, the gas will not ignite. If you have too much air, the gas will not ignite. You have to have between about 86% air to 94% of air mixed with a certain gas volume to get the gas to ignite. Once ignited, the ignition temperature of natural gas is about 1,200° F.

In a conventional gas furnace with a natural draft, air is mixed with the gas initially for combustion. This air is called the primary air. Primary air is controlled by the air shutters at the front of the burner assembly.

The remainder of the air mixture comes from the air that actually surrounds the flames inside the combustion chamber. This air is called the secondary air. The secondary air (the air around the flames) and the primary air (the air drawn into the burners) combine to make up the total combustion air.

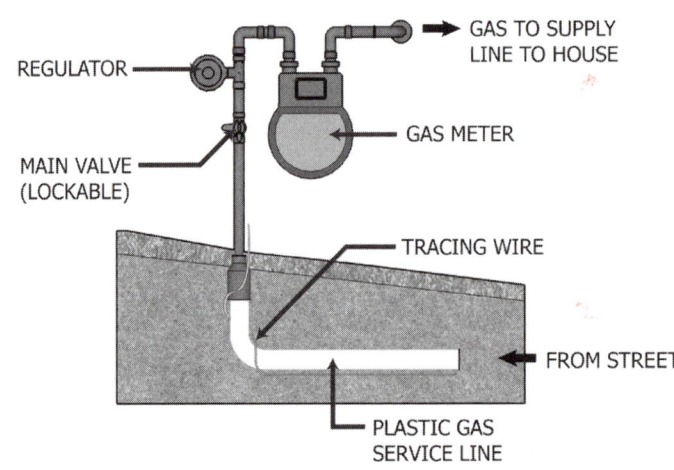

GAS SERVICE LINE AND OUTDOOR METER

REGULATOR

MAIN VALVE
(LOCKABLE)

GAS TO SUPPLY
LINE TO HOUSE

GAS METER

TRACING WIRE

FROM STREET

PLASTIC GAS
SERVICE LINE

## Gas Meter

A gas meter is a device that measures the volume of gas entering a building. Gas meters are used at residential and light commercial buildings. They are owned by the local gas company. Several different designs and types of gas meters are in use today. The meter may be found inside or outside the building. Most modern codes require the meter to be located outside because it is safer and more convenient for gas company personnel to monitor.

You are not required to inspect the gas meter. Many inspectors include a check of the gas meter in their inspection. You may decide to include in your report the description of the gas meter's location, and confirmation of the main valve being present.

Some inspectors inspect the meter for its visible condition, which may include the following:

- rust;
- peeling paint;
- physical/mechanical damage;
- ice/frost;

- inadequate access;

- possible gas leak;

- tilting; and

- poor installation.

### GAS SHUT OFF VALVES

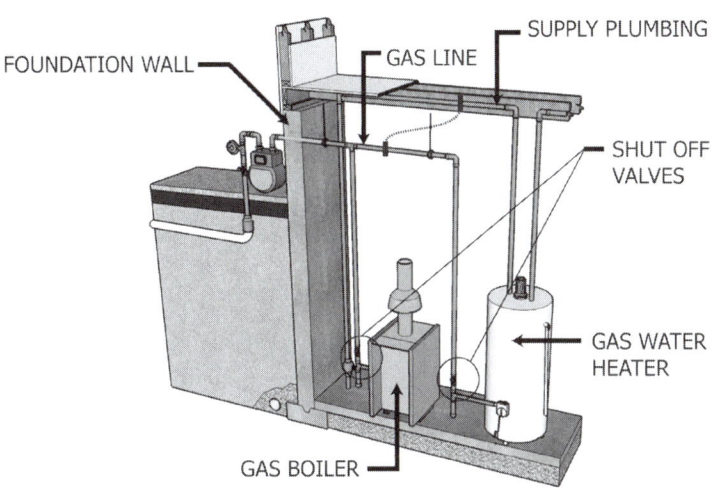

At a gas meter, check for the main valve. The main gas valve at the meter turns off the gas supply to the meter. There should be a way to lock the valve in either the "on" or "off" position. The meter and valve must be readily accessible. A meter may have a pressure regulator that adjusts the gas pressure that enters the building.

The gas service line from the street to the gas meter may be made of plastic. The plastic gas service line should be around 15 inches below ground level, but this may vary, depending on your jurisdiction. You should not see the plastic gas service line above the ground's surface. You may see a pipe (a metal riser) coming out of the ground and connecting to the gas meter. You may see a small wire wrapped around the service line that comes out of the ground next to the meter. This is called the tracer wire.

Rust on the gas meter is usually only a surface condition and not a major defect.

Look for gas meters that are located in areas where they could be damaged by impact. Gas meters should not be installed in driveways, carports or parking areas without steel posts or some other type of barrier installed to protect them against impact.

If the gas is in the "off" position, it is likely that a plumber or the gas company has turned the gas off. The gas could be shut off temporarily if there is an appliance inside the building that has been flagged or red-tagged as being unsafe to operate. If the gas is turned off, do not turn it on. You are not required to turn on and operate gas valves.

Gas meters covered with ice, frost or snow may simply be located under a roof edge that drops snow and ice on top of them. Gas meters should not be covered with ice or snow. They should not be located directly below the drip line of a roof's edge.

Gas meters should be readily accessible. You may find gas meters hidden under dense vegetation, or located in undesirable areas, including under decks or porches. Some building standards require that gas meters be installed with adequate clearance from combustible materials, from sources of ignition, and from the drip line of a roof edge.

Most codes prevent meters from being installed in unvented locations and crawlspaces.

## Gas Piping

The gas piping installed before the meter (and the meter itself) is usually the responsibility of the gas company. The gas piping installed after the meter is usually the responsibility of the homeowner.

The most common gas piping material is black iron. Copper, brass and stainless steel tubing are also used. If the gas piping is copper, then it should be of Type K, L or GP. Underground piping is usually Type K.

You may see corrugated stainless steel tubing (CSST). CSST was approved for residential use in 1988 by the National Fuel Gas Code. It is a method of supplying natural gas to fireplaces, furnaces, cooktops, clothes dryers, and any other gas appliance. However, some jurisdictions do not permit its use.

## COPPER TUBING FOR GAS PIPING

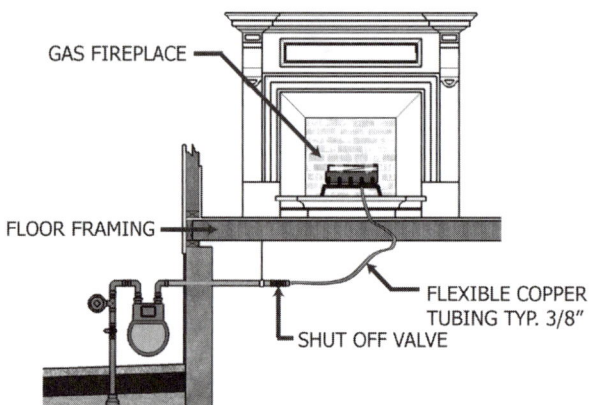

GAS FIREPLACE

FLOOR FRAMING

FLEXIBLE COPPER TUBING TYP. 3/8"

SHUT OFF VALVE

## TEFLON TAPE AT CONNECTIONS

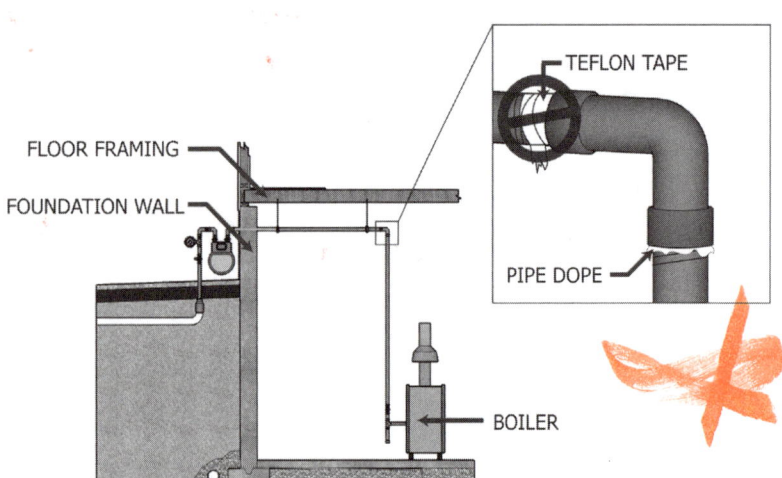

FLOOR FRAMING

FOUNDATION WALL

TEFLON TAPE

PIPE DOPE

BOILER

Most jurisdictions do not permit flexible gas pipes to go through walls, floors or ceilings. They cannot be concealed. They are limited in length. And the shut-off valve cannot be located in a different room than the appliance unless it is clearly labeled. Gas pipes should not pass through ducts.

Teflon® tape is not recommended for use at pipe connections. Pipe dope is preferred.

Most jurisdictions do not allow the use of gas piping as a way to ground the electrical service. We do not want to rely on the gas piping as the primary means of grounding the electrical service. Bonding the gas pipes to the electrical grounding system is a requirement in most jurisdictions. This bonding is usually done by connecting the gas piping to the water supply piping that is near the water heater. This is assuming that the water pipes are grounded.

Gas piping should be adequately supported. Check the floor for broken or loose support devices or brackets. Piping should not support other piping.

## GAS APPLIANCE CONNECTORS

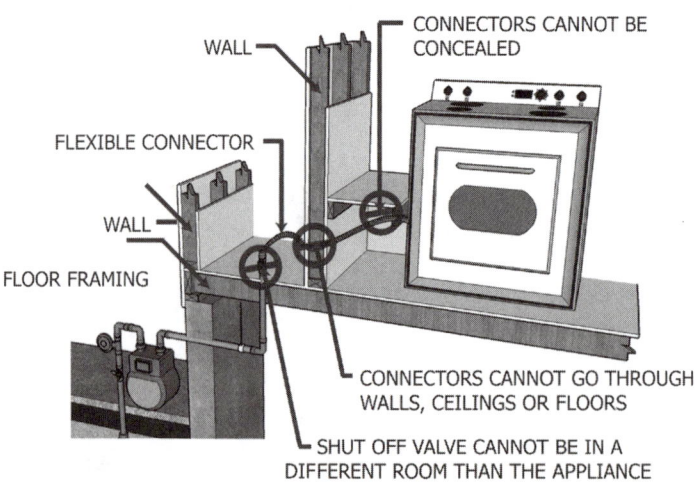

WALL

CONNECTORS CANNOT BE CONCEALED

FLEXIBLE CONNECTOR

WALL

FLOOR FRAMING

CONNECTORS CANNOT GO THROUGH WALLS, CEILINGS OR FLOORS

SHUT OFF VALVE CANNOT BE IN A DIFFERENT ROOM THAN THE APPLIANCE

BONDING THE GAS PIPING

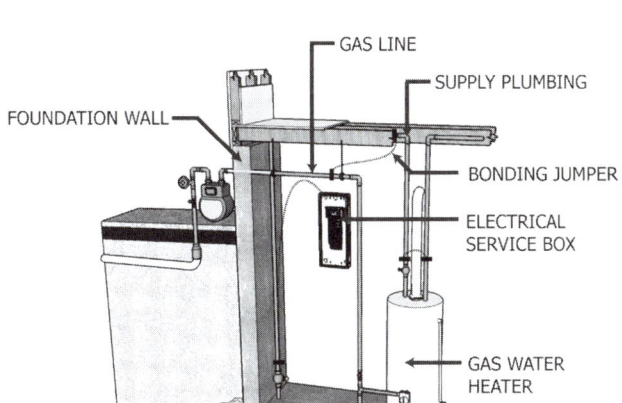

GAS PIPING SUPPORT

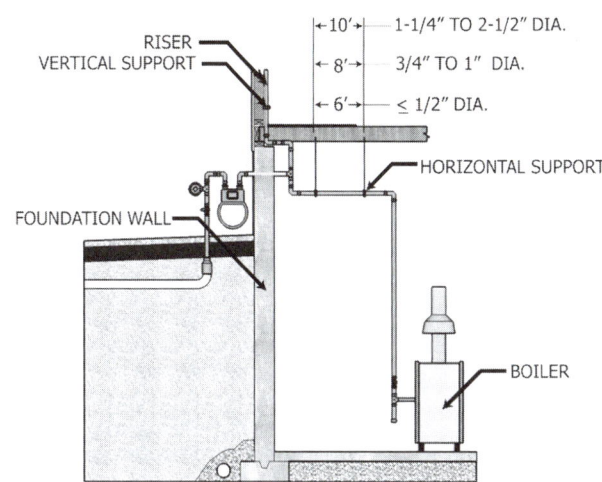

## Gas Leak

If there is a gas leak, you may smell it. The leak could be coming from a valve or a loose connection. As part of your inspection protocol, you could use a combustible gas analyzer to sniff for gas leaks. Using this type of instrument is not required by the Standards of Practice. If you smell a gas leak, contact the utility company immediately.

## Galvanized Steel

Black steel is commonly used inside a residential property to carry natural gas. Galvanized steel is not used because the zinc coating may flake and clog the line or the appliance. Try not to be confused by the appearance of the pipes. A gas pipe may appear to be a water supply pipe, and vice versa. If copper is permitted, both the water and the gas piping may be copper. Special identification of the lines in your jurisdiction may be required or recommended.

DRIP LEG

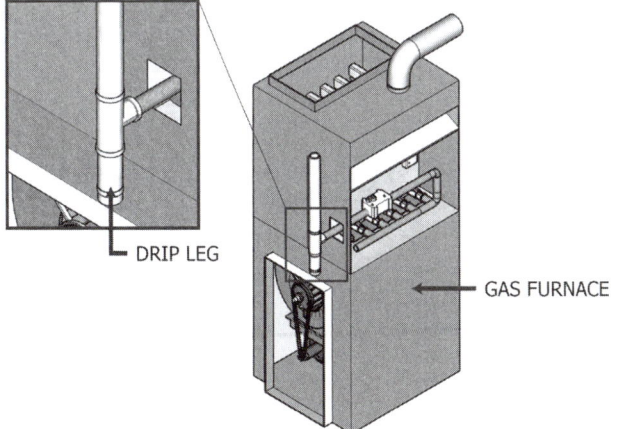

## Drip Leg

The drip leg (sediment trap or dirt leg) should be installed at the heating system. Look for the drip leg at the bottom of the vertical pipe that leads to the gas heating system. The debris that floats in the gas will drop into the drip or dirt leg before entering the vulnerable components of the heating system, such as the gas valve.

## Gas Shut-Off Valve

A gas shut-off valve should be installed adjacent to the heating system. With some exceptions, every gas appliance should have a readily accessible gas shut-off valve installed adjacent to the appliance. The inability to shut off the gas to a heating system would be dangerous. A shut-off valve is needed in order to safely perform maintenance and servicing of the system.

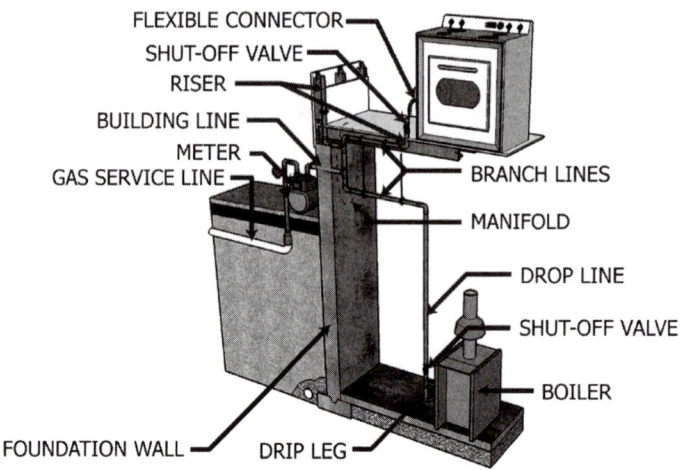

GAS PIPING TERMINOLOGY

FLEXIBLE CONNECTOR
SHUT-OFF VALVE
RISER
BUILDING LINE
METER
GAS SERVICE LINE
BRANCH LINES
MANIFOLD
DROP LINE
SHUT-OFF VALVE
BOILER
FOUNDATION WALL
DRIP LEG

# Combustion Fundamentals

Combustion involves the burning of a fuel that produces heat energy. Combustion requires an adequate supply of air called combustion air. For successful combustion, there must be a source of fuel, oxygen and ignition.

Burning a natural gas can be explained by the general equation:

$$CH_4 + 3O_2 = Heat + CO_2 + 2H_2O + O_2,$$

where:

$CH_4$ = 1 cubic foot of methane gas (natural gas),

$3O_2$ = 3 cubic feet of oxygen,

Heat = 1027 BTUs of energy produced from the chemical reaction,

$2H_2O$ = 2 cubic feet of water vapor,

$CO_2$ = 1 cubic foot of carbon dioxide, and

$O_2$ = 1 cubic foot of excess oxygen.

Natural gas is about 85 to 90% methane ($CH_4$). Burning natural gas ($CH_4$) with oxygen yields carbon dioxide ($CO_2$) and water vapor ($2H_2O$) and heat. This is referred to as complete combustion.

In reality, air is the source of oxygen ($O_2$), and in the air, oxygen is mixed with some nitrogen. The resultant flue gas from the combustion will contain some nitrogen.

Combustion is never complete (or perfect). In combustion exhaust gases, both unburned carbon (as soot) and carbon compounds (CO and others) will be present. Also, because air is the oxidant, some nitrogen will be oxidized into various nitrogen oxides ($NO_X$).

The formula for incomplete combustion in a gas-fired furnace is:

$$CH_4 + 3O_2 = Heat + 2H_2O + CO (+/- O_2).$$

The exhaust gasses can also include chemical combinations. Since the natural gas is burned with air, which contains 21% oxygen, 78% nitrogen and 1% trace gases, the exhaust can also include carbon monoxide (CO) and oxides of nitrogen ($NO_X$; nitrogen + oxygen), and if sulfur is present in the fuel, sulfur dioxide (SO2; sulfur + oxygen).

## Dew Point Temperature

The dew point temperature is the temperature below which the water vapor contained in the flue gas will turn into a condensate (a liquid). This is often referred to as condensation. For temperatures below the dew point temperature, moisture exists. For temperatures above the dew point temperature, vapor exists. If the chimney or venting material falls below the dew point temperature, condensation will occur in the flue. The dew point temperature can be measured if a technician sees indications of condensation occurring at a non-condensing appliance.

## Combustion Air

Roughly 15 cubic feet of air are needed to burn 1 cubic foot of natural gas. Gas furnaces also need draft air (or dilution air) to maintain a draft of the combustion gases. Another 15 cubic feet of air

COMBUSTION AIR

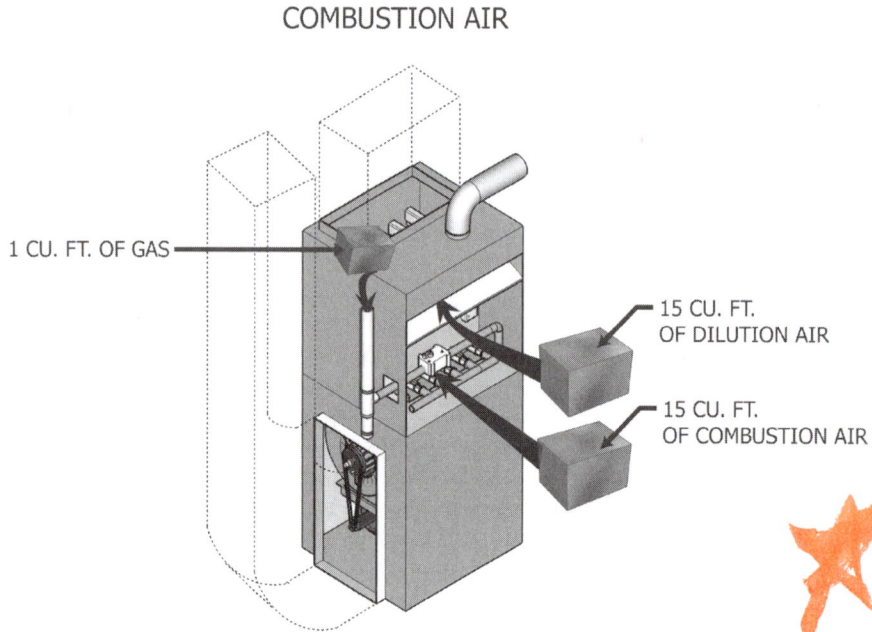

1 CU. FT. OF GAS

15 CU. FT.
OF DILUTION AIR

15 CU. FT.
OF COMBUSTION AIR

is needed for every cubic foot of natural gas. This air helps with a chimney draft. Therefore, a conventional low-efficiency, standing-pilot gas furnace requires about 30 cubic feet of air (15 dilution plus 15 combustion) for every cubic foot of gas burned.

If combustion air is inadequately supplied to a gas furnace, carbon monoxide will likely be produced. Carbon monoxide can be lethal.

## Draft Types

There are three types of burners relative to the draft. They are:

- natural-draft burners;
- induced-draft burners; and
- forced-draft burners.

Natural draft refers to the burners of a conventional low-efficiency gas furnace. This type of burner is also called an atmospheric burner. With natural draft, we need to keep the chimney hot enough to get those combustion gases out of the chimney. Natural draft burners have no draft fan.

A forced draft describes a furnace that has a fan that blows air into the combustion chamber through the heat exchanger and out through the venting system. All oil burners and some gas furnaces use forced draft. Forced draft has the fan before the burner.

NATURAL DRAFT

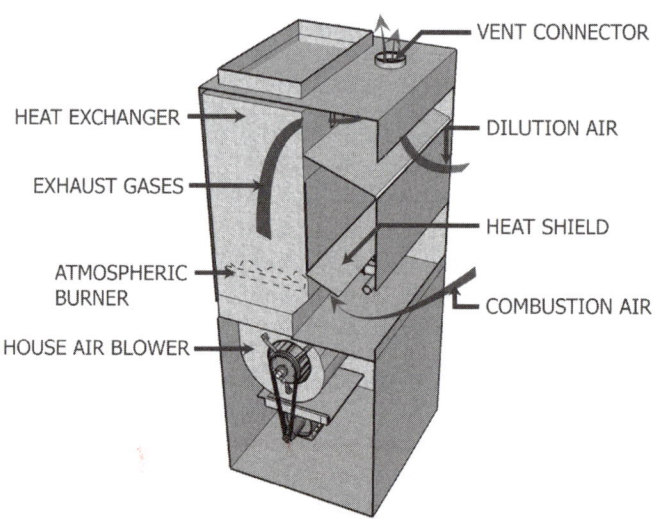

VENT CONNECTOR

HEAT EXCHANGER

DILUTION AIR

EXHAUST GASES

HEAT SHIELD

ATMOSPHERIC BURNER

COMBUSTION AIR

HOUSE AIR BLOWER

An induced draft uses a blower fan to pull air into the burner through the combustion chamber and exchanger. The fan is located on the exhaust side of the exchanger. It also blows the flue gases out through the vent connector pipe. When the induced fan is operating, there is a negative pressure inside the heat exchanger. Induced-draft fans are also called exhaust blowers or power vents. Induced draft has a fan after the exchanger and before the vent pipe. Induced-draft fans are common on mid-efficiency and high-efficiency furnaces.

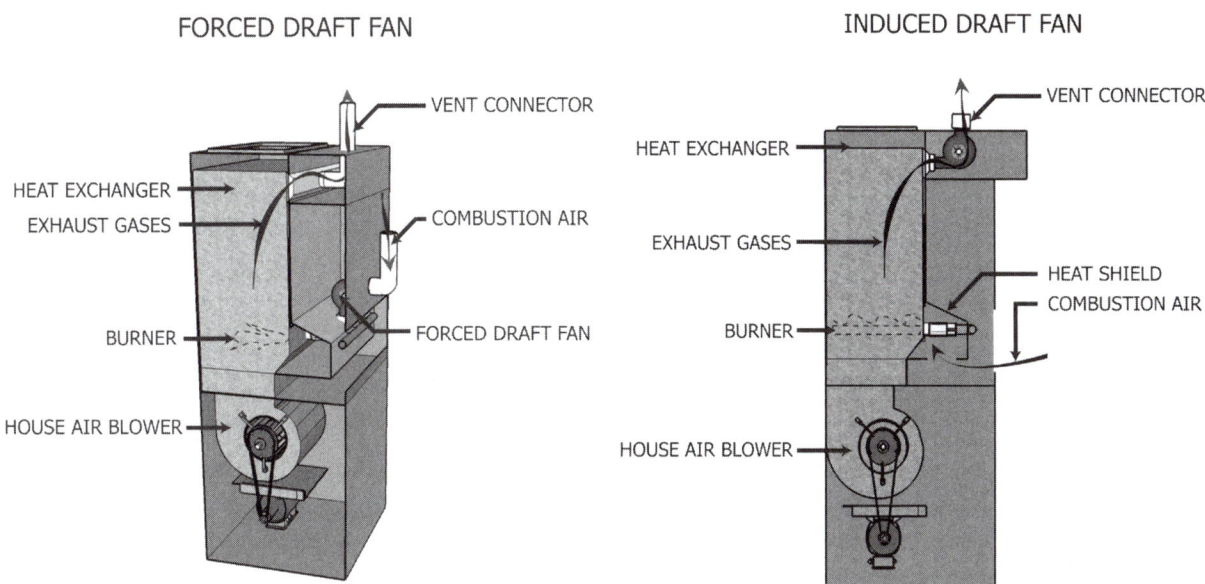

FORCED DRAFT FAN

INDUCED DRAFT FAN

## Draft

Draft refers to the flow of gases through the heat-generating equipment, beginning with the introduction of air at the burner. Once combustion occurs, the heated gas leaves the combustion chamber, passes the heat exchanger, and exits the exhaust stack. The draft may be natural and the combustion air is pulled in by buoyant heated gases venting up the stack. Or the draft may be mechanical and the air is pushed or pulled through the system by a fan.

Adequate draft is typically tested by a technician by measuring the pressure in the exhaust stack. The manufacturer of the fuel-burning equipment provides specifications for the required draft pressure and locations for making the draft measurement. Typical draft pressures are in the range of −0.5 to 0.5 inches of water column.

Excessive draft can prevent heat transfer to the system and increase the flue temperature if the excess air percentage is not elevated. If the excess air increases from the high draft, the flue temperature will decrease. Low draft pressures can cause temperatures in the flue to decrease, allowing water vapor to condense in the flue, forming acid and damaging the system.

## Backdraft

The lack of dilution air (the air used for draft) may cause a condition of backdraft at the furnace. Backdraft occurs when the combustion gases are not drafting or rising up through the chimney but are, instead, coming backward into the living area of the building. This is a hazardous situation, since carbon monoxide could be entering the dwelling.

Backdraft can be caused by various conditions, including:

- inadequate dilution air;
- flue restriction or blockage;
- chimney downdraft;
- exhaust fans causing draft and pressure problems within the building; and
- improper chimney or flue connector size.

## Confined Space and Combustion Air

If the volume of space where the appliance is located is less than 50 cubic feet of space per 1,000 BTUs per hour of aggregate input of the appliance, then it is considered a confined space.

> **50 cubic feet = 2.5 feet x 2.5 feet x 8 feet**

In unconfined spaces in buildings, infiltration may be adequate to provide air for combustion, ventilation and dilution of flue gases. However, in buildings of tight construction — for example, doors and windows that have weatherstripping, walls that are heavily insulated, openings that are caulked, floors and walls with vapor barriers, etc. — additional air may need to be provided.

## Solution

Two permanent openings to adjacent spaces could be provided so that the combined volume of all spaces meets the requirements. If the building is sealed so tightly that infiltration air is not adequate for combustion, combustion air should then be obtained from outdoors.

## All Air from Inside the Dwelling

If all combustion air is taken from the inside of the dwelling, then two permanent openings should be installed. One opening should be within 12 inches of the top and one opening should be within 12 inches of the bottom of the space. Each opening shall have a free area equal to a minimum of 1 square inch per 1,000 BTU-per-hour input rating of all appliances installed within the space, but not less than 100 square inches.

## All Air from Outdoors

If all combustion air is taken from the outdoor air, then one opening should be within 12 inches of the top and one opening should be within 12 inches of the bottom of the space. The openings are permitted to connect to spaces directly communicating with the outdoor air, such as a ventilated crawlspace or ventilated attic space. Each opening should have a free area of at least 1 square inch per 4,000 BTUs per hour of total input rating of all appliances in the space when using vertical ducts, or 2,000 BTUs per hour if using horizontal ducts.

## Louvers

In calculating the free area of a combustion air opening fitted with louvers, the inspector should note that metal louvers obstruct about 25% of the opening, and wooden louvers obstruct 75% of it.

# Furnace Fundamentals

A general home inspection includes inspecting, identifying and describing the heating system.

In order to perform an inspection according to the InterNACHI® Standards of Practice, an inspector must apply the knowledge of what s/he understands about the different types of residential heating systems. In order to fully inspect and identify a particular heating system, describe its heating method, and identify any material defects observed, an inspector should be able to explain and discuss with their client:

- the heating system;
- its heating method;
- its type or identification;
- how the heating system operates;
- how to maintain it; and
- the common problems that may be found.

The inspector must be able to thoroughly examine a heating system, understand how a particular heating system operates, and analyze and draw conclusions as to its apparent condition. An inspector should also be able to justify his/her observations, opinions and recommendations that s/he has written in the inspection report.

## Furnace

Let's focus on the fundamentals of a particular heating system called a furnace. There are many ways to inspect, identify and describe the different types of furnaces that may be found at a property using non-invasive, visual-only inspection techniques. It is up to the inspector's judgment as to how detailed the inspection and report will be. For example, the inspector is not required to determine the capacity or BTU of the inspected heating system, but many inspectors record that detailed information in their reports.

The American Society of Heating, Refrigerating and Air-Conditioning Engineers (ASHRAE) defines a furnace as a "complete heating unit for transferring heat from fuel being burned to the air supplied to a heating system." Another definition of a furnace is "a self-enclosed, fuel-burning unit for heating air by transfer of combustion through metal directly to the air." Taking these two definitions into consideration, there are two basic characteristics of a furnace:

- there is a fuel used to produce combustion; and
- heat is transferred to the interior air.

Note that air –- not water or steam -– is used as the medium to convey the heat. This characteristic distinguishes warm-air heating systems from other types of heating systems.

Let's look at how to identify and describe some warm-air heating systems known as furnaces.

Most modern furnaces are commonly referred to as central heating systems. The furnace is typically centralized within the structure. The furnace is used as the main, central warm-air heating system. The heat of the furnace is forced (or rises) through a system of ducts or pipes to other areas and rooms within the structure. The furnace does not necessarily need to be centrally located within the structure if the furnace is a forced warm-air system.

Furnaces that have no distribution ducts or pipes are used in some heating applications. They are limited in the size of the area that they can heat. They are installed within the room or area to be heated and have no way to distribute the heat to other places.

## Identification and Description of Furnaces

There are several ways to identify and describe a furnace using non-invasive, visual-only inspection techniques, as required by the InterNACHI® Standards of Practice.

Furnaces can be identified and described by:

- fuel type;
- distribution;
- air flow;
- gravity or forced;
- efficiency; and
- ignition.

## Fuel Type

One way to identify and describe a furnace is based on the type of fuel used to produce heat.

Based on fuel type, one can classify a furnace as:

- gas-fired;
- oil-fired;
- coal-burning;
- wood-burning;
- multi-fuel; or
- electric.

Fossil fuels are used to produce combustion in the first five types listed above. The last one uses electricity. Whether or not electricity can be considered a fuel is not important here, since an electric furnace functions in the same manner as the fossil-burning furnaces. The electric furnace heats air and distributes it. According to the InterNACHI® Standards, an inspector is required to describe the energy source in the report.

## Distribution

The inspector is also required to describe the heating method. One way to do that is to identify the method for how the air is distributed throughout the house. Furnaces can be identified and described or classified by the way the air is distributed. There are two broad categories:

- gravity warm-air furnaces; and
- forced warm-air furnaces.

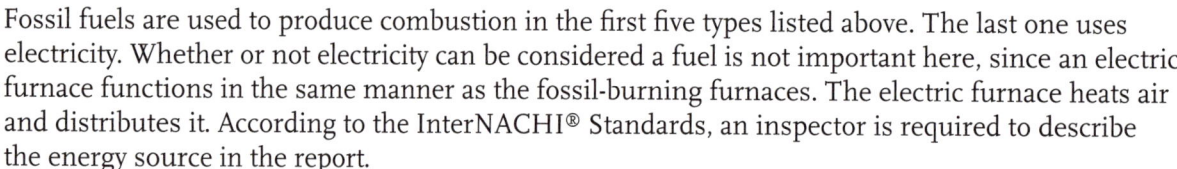

Gravity warm-air furnaces rely primarily on gravity for circulating the heated air. Warm air is lighter than cool air and will rise and move through ducts and pipes. After releasing its heat, the air becomes cooler and heavier. The air drops down the structure through return registers to the furnace, where it is heated again, and the cycle continues. The very earliest types of furnaces were gravity-type furnaces. Many of these had a blower fan installed to move the heated air. They have been replaced by modern forced warm-air furnaces.

## Air Flow

Forced warm-air furnaces can be identified and described by how the air flows through the heating unit in relation to the warm-air outlet and the return-air inlet locations on the furnace. There are three types of forced warm-air furnaces related to air flow:

- upflow (highboy or lowboy);
- downflow; and
- horizontal.

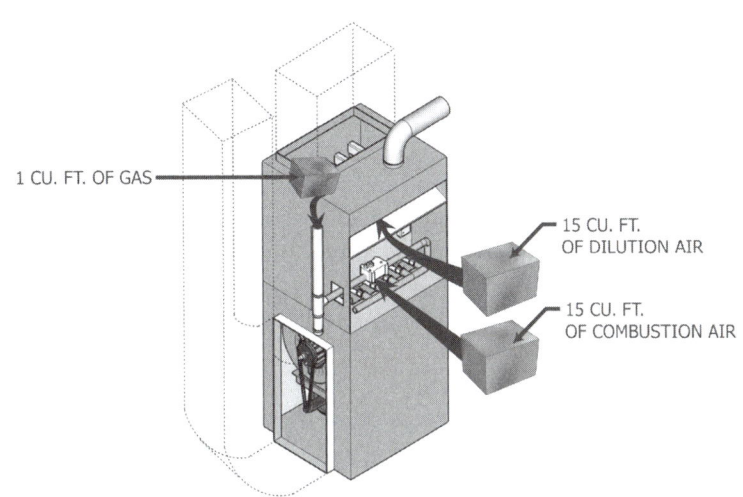

COMBUSTION AIR

1 CU. FT. OF GAS

15 CU. FT. OF DILUTION AIR

15 CU. FT. OF COMBUSTION AIR

Furnace manufacturers commonly use the terms "upflow," "downflow" and "horizontal" in their literature that describes their products, including their marketing materials, and in their installation and operation manuals.

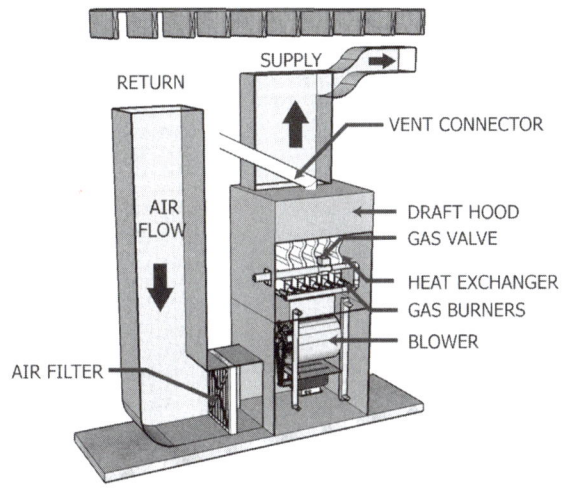

UPFLOW GAS FURNACE

RETURN

SUPPLY

VENT CONNECTOR

AIR FLOW

DRAFT HOOD

GAS VALVE

HEAT EXCHANGER

GAS BURNERS

BLOWER

AIR FILTER

## Upflow Highboy

On a typical upflow highboy furnace, the warm-air outlet is located at the top of the furnace, so warm air discharges out of the top. The return-air inlet is located at the bottom or sides of the furnace. A cooling unit is usually added to the top of an upflow furnace. A typical upflow highboy furnace stands no higher than 6 feet and can occupy a floor space of 6 square feet (2 x 3 feet).

## Upflow Lowboy

An upflow lowboy furnace is designed for low clearances. Both the warm-air outlet and return-air inlet are located at the top of the furnace. The lowboy is usually installed in a basement where most of the ductwork is located above the heating unit. This compact heating unit typically stands no higher than 4 feet. It is usually longer from front to back than either the upflow highboy or downflow furnaces.

## Downflow

A downflow furnace is also referred to as a counterflow furnace or a down-draft furnace. Warm air discharges out of the bottom of a downflow furnace, and the return-air inlet is located at the top. The downflow furnace is

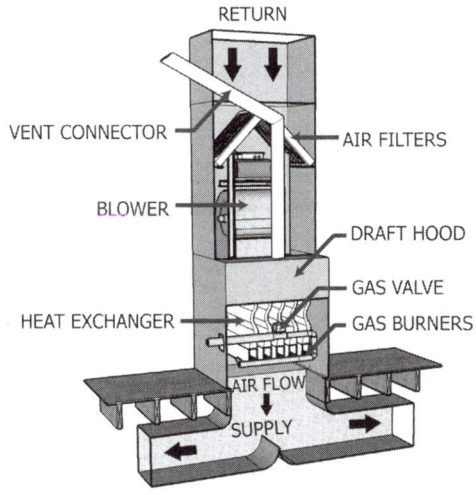

DOWNFLOW GAS FURNACE

RETURN

VENT CONNECTOR

AIR FILTERS

BLOWER

DRAFT HOOD

HEAT EXCHANGER

GAS VALVE

GAS BURNERS

AIR FLOW

SUPPLY

usually installed when most of the duct or pipe distribution system is located below the furnace. The ducts may be embedded in a concrete floor slab or suspended in a crawlspace below the heating unit. The downflow furnace is similar in dimensions to the upflow, but the warm-air outlet is located at the bottom instead of the top.

## Horizontal

A horizontal furnace is designed primarily for installations with low, restricted space, such as a crawlspace or attic. A typical horizontal furnace is about 2 feet wide by 2 feet tall and 5 feet long.

## Gravity Warm-Air Furnace

A gravity warm-air furnace's operation is based on the principles that warm air is

HORIZONTAL GAS-FIRED FURNACE

lighter than cool air, and warm air rises. In a gravity warm-air furnace, warm air may rise through ducts or pipes. After releasing its heat, the air becomes cooler and heavier. The air drops down the structure through return registers to the furnace, where it is heated again. The air is circulated through the house in this manner.

The very earliest type of furnaces were gravity warm-air furnaces. They were popular from the first half of the 19th century to the early 1970s. Some had a blower fan installed to move the heated air. But the primary way the air moved through the house relied on how gravity affected the different weights of warm and cool air. Gravity warm-air furnaces were sometimes described as "octopus" furnaces because of their appearance, with all of the pipes coming out of the centrally located heating unit. Most of these gravity furnaces are obsolete. If an inspector finds one still in use, it is likely at the end of its service life.

A gravity warm-air furnace can be described in one of the following three ways:

- a gravity warm-air furnace without a fan;
- a gravity warm-air furnace with an integral fan; or
- a gravity warm-air furnace with a booster fan.

A gravity warm-air furnace without a fan relies entirely on gravity and the different weights of air to circulate the air through the house. The air flow rate is slow. The air circulation and distribution of heated air is not efficient. It is all but impossible to effectively control the heat supplied to individual rooms of the house. An integral fan may be installed in the distribution ducts or pipes to reduce the internal resistance to air flow and increase air movement.

A booster fan is installed to do the same thing, but it does not interfere with air circulation when it is not in use. A booster fan may be a belt-driven type that rests on the floor and is attached to the outside of the heating unit.

Floor and space heaters operate using the same principles of gravity and air weights, as do gravity warm-air furnaces. However, they differ in that a floor or space heater is designed to provide heated air to a particular room or space and does not distribute air throughout the house.

## Warm Air Rises

When a certain amount of air is heated up, it expands and takes up more space. In other words, hot air is less dense than cold air. Any substance that is less dense than the fluid (gas or liquid) of its surroundings will float. Hot air floats on cold air because it is less dense, just as a piece of wood floats because it is less dense than water. Warm air weighs less than cool air.

## Pipeless Floor and Wall Furnaces

A pipeless floor furnace is a gravity warm-air heating system that is installed directly beneath a floor. One large grille is installed for the warm air to rise up through. A cool-air return is installed for air circulation. This type of furnace is sometimes considered a permanently installed room heater. A wall furnace is installed in the wall and is also considered a permanently installed room heater. Some of these units have blower fans, but most operate on the principle of gravity for air circulation.

A common wall furnace is a type that is installed on a wall, in a closet, or in a wall recess. Wall furnaces are usually gas- or oil-fired vertical units. There are upflow and downflow wall furnaces with grilles at the bottom and top of the vertical unit.

## Furnace Maintenance

Many property inspectors look for and report on indications of delayed maintenance. Furnace maintenance is a very important part of the efficient operation of a warm-air heating system. Furnace maintenance should never be neglected. The furnace manufacturer provides recommendations for proper maintenance in their installation and operation manuals. With proper maintenance, the life of the furnace will be extended, its efficiency will improve, and the cost to operate it will be reduced. Maintaining a furnace includes cleaning and/or replacing the air filter on a regular basis. Furnaces should be periodically serviced by a technician. A maintenance schedule should be used and posted near the furnace. The maintenance schedule should have dates, maintenance comments, descriptions of repairs performed, and contact information for the local technician who works on the furnace.

# Quiz #4

1. Burning natural gas with oxygen yields carbon dioxide, water vapor, and _____.

     ☐ refrigerant
     ☑ heat
     ☐ cooling

2. T/F: A natural draft unit has a draft fan.

     ☐ True
     ☑ False

3. There are two broad categories that describe furnace heating systems: gravity warm-air furnaces; and _____ warm-air furnaces.

     ☐ natural
     ☑ forced
     ☐ convective

4. A(n) _____ furnace is also referred to as a counterflow furnace or a down-draft furnace.

     ☐ upflow
     ☑ downflow
     ☐ horizontal

**Answer Key is on page 117.**

# Warm-Air Heating Systems

Warm-air heating systems use air as the heat-conveying medium that carries heat from the system to the rooms and spaces of the dwelling. Air as the heat-conveying medium is the distinguishing characteristic noted by inspectors to identify and describe the particular type of system. The warm-air heating system is usually (but not always) centrally located in the structure.

The following fuels can be used in a warm-air heating system:

- fuel oil (No. 2);
- natural gas;
- propane;
- coal;
- electricity;
- wood;
- kerosene; and
- pellets.

A warm-air heating system operates as follows:

1. Cool air enters the furnace.
2. The furnace heats the air.
3. The warm air begins to rise.
4. The air is distributed either by simply rising up through the house (as in a gravity warm-air furnace), or by a fan through ducts or pipes (as in a forced warm-air furnace).
5. The warm air gives off its heat, gets cooler and heavier, and returns to the furnace, where it is re-heated and re-circulated.

A warm-air heating system is one in which air is heated by a furnace and then distributed to the rest of the structure by gravity or by the use of a centrifugal fan. If gravity is employed, then the warm-air heating system is referred to as a gravity warm-air heating system. If the movement of air relies primarily on a fan or some other mechanical means for circulation, then the warm-air heating system is referred to as a forced warm-air heating system.

Remember:

- If gravity is used, it's a gravity warm-air heating system.
- If a fan is used, it's a forced warm-air heating system.

It is possible to confuse one type with the other. Some gravity warm-air systems use fans to assist in air movement and circulation, so one system may be mistaken for the other when attempting to describe it. One of the easiest ways for inspectors to identify and describe a particular heating system is based on how the air is circulated — by gravity or by a fan.

## Gravity Warm-Air Heating Systems

A gravity warm-air heating system is a furnace with a means of supplying warm air and returning cool air that relies primarily on gravity to move the air. The system consists of a furnace and some ducts or pipes. Warm air rises, and cool air falls. The weight per unit-volume of air decreases as its temperature increases. And, conversely, the weight per unit-volume of air increases as its temperature decreases.

The furnace heats the air, and the air gets lighter and rises out of the heating system. Cool air enters the heating system and pushes or displaces the warm, rising air. The warm air rises up through warm-air ducts or pipes (often called stacks) that are inside the walls. The warm air rises up through the building. The warm air enters a room through the supply registers on the wall or floor. The cool air falls out of the room and may return through a return grille, traveling back through return ducts to the heating system. Some houses with old gravity heating systems may not have a lot of ducts and pipes but may have large openings covered with iron grates or grilles in the floors that allow the cool air to fall down through the building. The cool air simply falls back to the furnace –- hence, the name gravity warm-air heating system.

The efficiency of the air circulation in a house with a gravity warm-air heating system depends on the temperature difference between the warm air rising and the cool air falling. The greater the temperature difference, the greater the speed that the air will circulate. Also, air circulation in a gravity warm-air heating system is greatly affected by air filtering. An air filter can resist and almost block the air flow in a gravity system. You may find that an integral fan has been installed to overcome resistance to air flow.

## Forced Warm-Air Heating Systems

A forced warm-air heating system consists of a furnace, a blower fan, controls, a duct distribution system, and supply and return registers. The heating system warms the air, and the air is forced through ducts or pipes into rooms throughout the building. The cool air returns through the ducts back to the furnace, where it is re-heated. And the cycle begins again.

Some large homes have balancing problems. Certain rooms may feel colder than the rest of the house. This problem can be solved in a few ways. One is by dividing the heating system into two separate zones, with each controlled by its own thermostat. You may find a motorized damper installed in the duct system that is controlled by a thermostat. Zoning equipment can be expensive. Usually, a system can be balanced manually by adjusting the supply dampers installed inside the main supply ducts, and by using the dampers at the warm-air outlets (lever-controlled dampers, floor diffusers, or registers).

## Warm-Air Furnace

Most modern furnaces are commonly referred to as central heating systems. The furnace is centralized within the structure. The furnace is used as the main, central warm-air heating system. The heat of the furnace is forced or rises through a system of ducts or pipes to other areas and rooms in the structure. The furnace does not necessarily need to be centrally located within the structure if the furnace is a forced warm-air system.

There are some furnaces that have no distribution ducts or pipes. They are limited in the size of the area that they can heat. They are installed within the room or area to be heated and have no means to distribute the heat to other places.

## Identification and Description of Furnaces

There are several ways to identify and describe a furnace using non-invasive, visual-only inspection techniques, as required by the InterNACHI® Standards of Practice.

Furnaces can be identified and described by:

- fuel type;
- distribution;
- air flow;
- gravity or forced air;
- efficiency; and
- ignition.

## Fuel Type

One way to identify and describe a furnace is based on the type of fuel it uses to produce heat. Based on its fuel type, a furnace can be classified as:

- gas-fired;
- oil-fired;
- coal-burning;
- wood-burning;
- multi-fuel; or
- electric.

Fossil fuels are used to produce combustion in the first five types. The last one uses electricity. Whether or not electricity can be considered a fuel is not important here, since an electric furnace functions in the same manner as the other fossil-burning furnaces. The electric furnace heats air and distributes it. According to the SOP, an inspector is required to describe the energy source in the report.

## Distribution

### AIR DISTRIBUTION SYSTEM

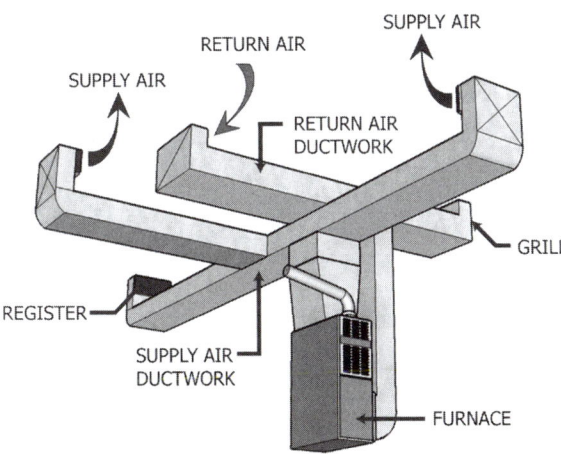

The inspector is also required to describe the heating method. One way to do that is to identify the method of how the air is distributed throughout the house. Furnaces can be identified and described or classified by the way the air is distributed. There are two broad categories:

- gravity warm-air furnaces; and
- forced warm-air furnaces.

To review, gravity warm-air furnaces rely primarily on gravity for circulating the heated air. Warm air is lighter than cool air and will rise and move through ducts or pipes. After releasing its heat, the air becomes cooler and heavier. The air drops down the structure through return registers and back to the furnace, where it is heated again, and the cycle continues. The very earliest type of furnace was a gravity-type. Many such furnaces had a blower fan installed to move the heated air. These have been replaced by modern, forced warm-air furnaces.

By modern comfort standards, gravity warm-air heating systems have many advantages but also many disadvantages. Gravity systems do not have blower fans, so they don't have good air circulation for adequate air conditioning, including good air-temperature control, humidity control, and air filtering.

## Advantages of Warm-Air Heating Systems

- It costs less to install than a hot-water or steam-heating system.

- Heat is delivered to the rooms relatively quickly.

- Heat delivery can be stopped quickly.

- Air filtering is easy to install.

- Humidity can be easily controlled.

- Air cooling (or air conditioning) can be easily installed.

- A forced warm-air system does not have to be centrally located.

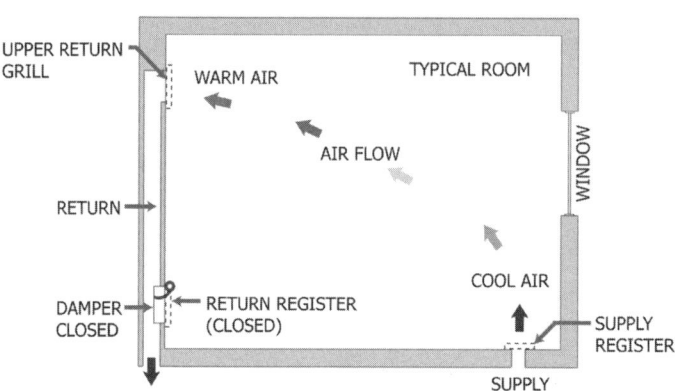

## Disadvantages of Warm-Air Heating Systems

- Gravity warm-air systems have to be centrally located at the lowest level of the structure.

- They are slow to respond to controls.

- Air movement is slow.

- Air filtering is restricted.

- Forced warm-air heating systems require blower fans, which sometimes make noise.

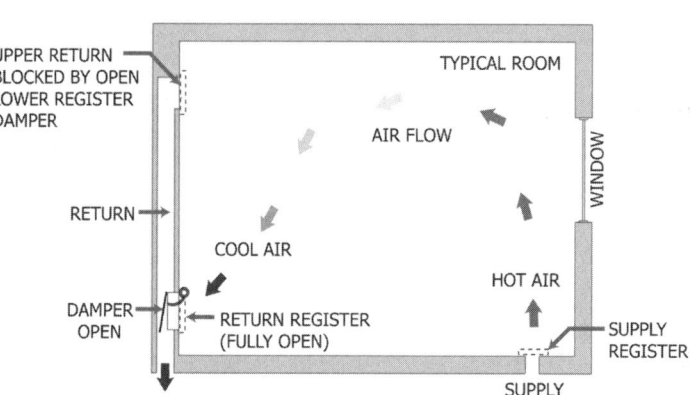

- The air movement may cause indoor air-quality issues because the air agitates dust and other particles.

- Cool-air return inlets and warm-air supply registers must not be blocked, which sometimes interferes with positioning of furniture. They also have some architectural design demands.

- Warm air is supplied in bursts of convection heat, which may cause the temperature in different rooms to vary.

# Ducts

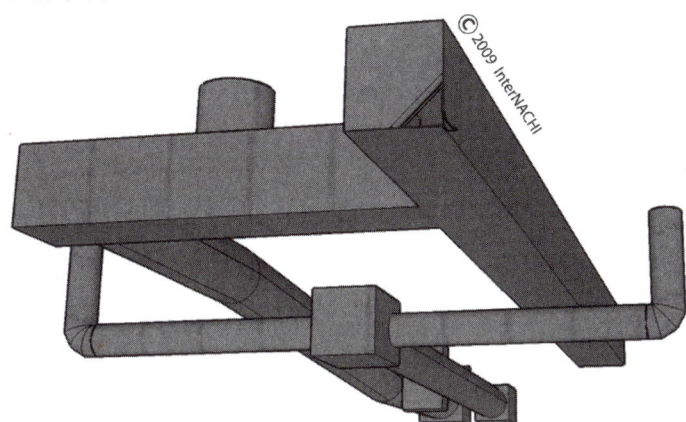

Duct systems for HVAC equipment should be installed in accordance with Manual D of the Indoor Environment and Energy Efficiency Association (ACCA), local building codes, and the manufacturer's recommendations. There are two general major categories for ducts: above-ground and underground ducts. Above-ground duct systems are commonly installed in homes built in North America.

Ducts must be sized properly for efficient and proper circulation of conditioned air. Restriction of the supply duct system is a rare problem. However, inadequately sized return duct systems are often found by home inspectors, particularly for heat pump systems. The International Residential Code (IRC) does not specifically describe duct requirements, but it relies on the ACCA Manual D and appliance manufacturers for installation recommendations and standards.

The maximum discharge temperature for ducts of a warm-air heating system is 250° F.

## Drywall

The use of gypsum material (drywall) for the construction of a return-air duct system or plenum is allowed, provided that the air temperature does not exceed 125° F. Gypsum board is a composite material commonly used to build air plenums, shafts, and spaces. Air temperatures greater than 125° F, will, over time, dry out the paper-facing material on the drywall and will lead to deterioration of the panel. Drywall can also deteriorate when exposed to moisture or condensation. For this reason, drywall must not be used with evaporative cooling equipment (or swamp coolers).

## Stud Wall Cavity

Stud wall cavities and the space between floor joists can be used as plenums, under several conditions:

- These spaces cannot be used for supply air.
- These spaces must not be part of a fire-resistance assembly.
- These spaces must not convey air from more than one floor level of a house.
- These spaces must be isolated from adjacent concealed spaces with fireblocking.
- These spaces in the outside walls of a house must not be used as air plenums.

## Plenum and Perimeter Duct Systems

Forced warm-air heating systems can be identified by the type of duct system installed. There are two broad classifications:

- perimeter duct systems; and
- plenum duct systems.

Perimeter and plenum systems (or extended plenum systems) are the two duct systems most commonly used at forced warm-air heating systems.

## Perimeter Duct System

If you are inspecting a perimeter duct system, you should find supply registers located around the exterior walls of the room at the floor area. The return registers may be located at the ceiling of the inside wall.

## Perimeter Loop and Perimeter Radial

There are two common types of perimeter duct systems: perimeter loop and perimeter radial. A perimeter loop duct system actually has a loop of duct or pipe that connects all of the exterior registers at the perimeter, outside the wall's outer edge. The ducts extend out from the centrally located heating system to a loop duct at the perimeter that connects all the supply registers. With a radial perimeter duct system, the ducts radiate out from a centralized location where the heating system is installed, and extends outward to the exterior walls where the supply registers are located. There is no loop duct at a radial perimeter system.

Perimeter loop warm-air heating systems are typically found in homes built on a concrete slab rather than those having a basement. In this system, round ducts are embedded in the slab.

## Plenum Duct System

If you are inspecting a plenum-duct system, then you should find a large rectangular duct that comes directly out of the heating system and runs in a straight line down the center of the basement, attic or ceiling. From the large rectangular plenum extension, you will find ducts branching out to all of the supply registers or heat-emitting units. The branching ducts are usually round, located between floor joists, and usually covered by a ceiling.

Plenum duct systems are often called extended plenum duct systems because the large rectangular duct extends directly out of the supply outlet (or main plenum) of the heating system. The extended plenum duct system is common in most modern residential forced warm-air heating systems.

## Duct Materials

Above-ground ducts can be made out of a variety of materials, including:

- plain steel;
- galvanized sheet metal;
- aluminum;
- copper;
- fiberglass;
- paper fiber; and
- vitrified clay tile.

Metal ducts are usually constructed of galvanized sheet steel.

Plain steel and galvanized sheet-metal cuts are about 0.0163 to 0.1419 inches thick. Aluminum and copper ducts are typically installed outside the building. Paper fiber and clay ducts are installed in concrete.

Underground ducts are made of approved concrete, clay, metal or plastic. The maximum duct temperature for plastic ducts is 150° F. Metal ducts should be protected from corrosion.

## Vibration Isolators

Vibration isolators should be installed between metal duct and the mechanical equipment. Isolators should be made of approved materials and should not be longer than 10 inches.

## Ducts in Garages

Ducts that are located in a garage, and ducts penetrating separation walls or ceilings between a garage and a living space of a house, must be designed and installed to prevent fire and smoke from entering the living spaces of the house. The penetration of the fire separation between a house and an attached garage must be protected. Code assumes that the 26-gauge steel duct will provide a significant impediment to the spread of fire from the garage to the house's interior.

HVAC systems that supply air to the living space of a house must not supply air to or return air from a garage. A furnace or air handler is prohibited from serving both the garage and living spaces. If a garage is conditioned, it must have an independent HVAC system. The garage could contain contaminants that would affect the indoor air quality of the living spaces.

## Return Air

Return air is typically partially or completely recirculated air; therefore, it is important to control from where the return air is taken.

Return air openings for HVAC systems must comply with the following:

- Openings must be located more than 10 feet measured in any direction from an open combustion chamber or draft hood of another appliance located in the same room or space.

- The amount of return air taken from any room or space must not exceed the flow rate of supply air delivered to that room or space.

- Return air must not be taken from a closet, bathroom, toilet room, kitchen, garage, mechanical room, boiler room, furnace room, or unconditioned attic.

TYPICAL SUPPLY AND RETURN REGISTER LOCATIONS

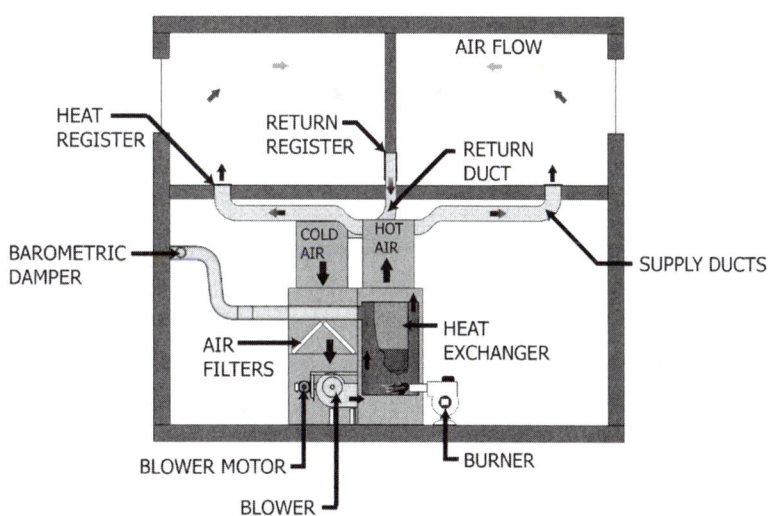

Returns should be located as far away as possible from the supply outlets. Returns are typically located at the bottom of walls near the center of the building.  Return grilles should be installed away from the furnace. If the return grille is too close to the furnace, problems with draft can be created, causing backdraft or flame rollout conditions.

## Duct Terms

In a forced warm-air heating system, the warm air comes out of the furnace in an area called the **furnace plenum** or **furnace hood**. An **extended plenum** duct system has a large rectangular duct connected to this plenum and extends out in a straight line. The duct between the furnace and the plenum is often called the **starting collar**. Ducts that carry warm air to a room are called **supply ducts**. Round or square supply ducts that are connected to and branch off the extended duct are called **side takeoffs**. These supply branches are connected to **register boots** or **elbows**. Changes in direction of the ducts are made by **angle ducts**. A large vertical duct or warm-air riser is sometimes called a **stack duct**. A warm-air supply duct that runs horizontally from the furnace plenum to a riser is called a **leader**. **Dampers** may be installed in ducts to control the amount of air moving through the duct. Dampers can be manually or automatically controlled. All of the ducts that carry cool air back to the furnace are called **return ducts**.

## Dampers

A damper is a device used to alter the volume of air passing through a confined cross-section by changing the size of the cross-sectional area.  It controls the air flow inside a duct or pipe by acting as a moveable obstruction.  There are volume dampers, splitter dampers, and squeeze dampers. Dampers can be manually or automatically controlled.

## Grilles, Registers and Diffusers

There are three general types of warm-air supply outlet devices:

- grilles;
- registers; and
- diffusers.

Grilles deflect the air up, down, and side to side, depending on the direction that the louvers are pointed.  Grilles are installed high or low on walls.  Floor grilles are commonly used in gravity warm-air systems.  They may have movable louvers, but this is rare.

Registers are similar to grilles, but registers have dampers to control the air flow.  They can be located on walls or floors.

Diffusers are typically formed in concentric cones or pyramids.  They can be located on walls and are usually found on ceilings.  Baseboard diffusers are used in perimeter forced warm-air heating systems.

## Integration

Central air conditioning units can be easily integrated with central heating systems using the same ductwork. This is an advantage of having ductwork installed for the heating and cooling systems of a house.

# Quiz #5

1. If you are inspecting a _____ duct system, you should find a large rectangular duct that comes directly out of the heating system and runs in a straight line down the center of the basement, attic or ceiling.

   ☒ plenum
   ☐ perimeter
   ☐ loop

2. T/F: Round or square supply ducts that are connected to and branch off the extended duct are called side takeoffs.

   ☒ True
   ☐ False

3. T/F: Diffusers are typically formed in concentric cones or pyramids.

   ☒ True
   ☐ False

**Answer Key is on page 118.**

# Gas Furnaces

There are many ways to describe different types of residential gas furnaces. Gas furnaces can be classified by:

- the direction of the air flowing through the heating unit;
- the heating efficiency of the unit; and
- the type of ignition system installed on the unit.

### Air Flow in Gas Furnaces

One way to identify and describe a gas furnace is by the direction of the air flowing through the heating unit, or the location of the warm-air outlet and the return-air inlet on the furnace. Gas furnaces can be described as upflow, downflow (counterflow), highboy, lowboy, and horizontal flow. Air can flow up through the furnace (upflow), down through the furnace (downflow), or across the furnace (horizontal). The arrangement of the furnace should not significantly affect its operation, or your inspection.

### BTU

Gas furnaces can be classified by their different capacities. A furnace's capacity can be described by its BTU output. The appropriate BTU is determined by the heating requirements of the structure, which is the amount of heat the system needs to produce in order to replace heat loss and provide the occupants with a satisfactory comfort level.

### AFUE

Furnaces can be identified and described by their heating efficiency. The energy efficiency of a natural gas furnace is measured by its annual fuel utilization efficiency (AFUE). The higher the AFUE rating, the more efficient the furnace. The U.S. government has established a minimum rating for furnaces of 78%. Mid-efficiency furnaces have AFUE ratings of 78 to 82%. High-efficiency furnaces have AFUE ratings of 88 to 97%. Old standing-pilot gas furnaces have AFUE ratings of 60 to 65%. Gravity warm-air furnaces can have efficiency ratings that are below 60%.

### BTU and Efficiency

BTU stands for British thermal unit. The BTU is a unit of energy. It is approximately the amount of energy needed to heat 1 pound of water by 1 degree Fahrenheit. One cubic foot of natural gas contains about 1,000 BTUs. A gas furnace that fires at a rate of 100,000 BTUs per hour will burn about 100 cubic feet of gas every hour.

There should be a data plate on a gas furnace. On that plate may be indicated the furnace's input and output capacities. For example, the data plate may say, "Input 100,000 BTU per hour." And it may also say, "Output 80,000 BTU per hour." While this furnace is running, about 20% of the heat generated is lost through the exhaust gases. The ratio of the output to the input BTU is 80,000 ÷ 100,000 = 80% efficiency. This is the "steady-state efficiency" of the furnace.

Steady-state efficiency measures how efficiently a furnace converts fuel to heat, once the furnace has warmed up and is running steadily. However, furnaces cycle off and on as they maintain their desired temperature. Furnaces typically don't operate as efficiently when they start up and cool down. As a result, steady-state efficiency is not as reliable an indicator of the overall efficiency of a furnace.

## AFUE and Efficiency

The AFUE is the most widely used measure of a furnace's heating efficiency. It measures the amount of heat delivered to the house compared to the amount of fuel that must be supplied to the furnace. Thus, a furnace that has an 80% AFUE rating converts 80% of the fuel that is supplied to heat. The other 20% is lost and wasted.

Note that the AFUE refers only to the unit's fuel efficiency and not its electricity usage. In 1992, the U.S. Department of Energy (DOE) required that all furnaces sold in the U.S. must have a minimum AFUE of 78%. Furnaces installed in mobile/manufactured homes are required to have a minimum AFUE of 75%.

The DOE's definition of AFUE is the measure of the seasonal or annual efficiency of a furnace or boiler. It takes into account the cyclic on/off operation and associated energy losses of the heating unit as it responds to changes in the load, which, in turn, are affected by changes in the weather and occupant controls.

## Ignition Type

A gas furnace can be identified and described by the type of ignition system it uses. The different types of ignition systems are:

- standing-pilot;
- intermittent-pilot or direct-spark; and
- hot-surface ignition.

Older gas furnaces have a standing-pilot light that is always burning. Modern furnaces with higher efficiency ratings are slowly replacing these older, conventional gas furnaces.

## Standing-Pilot

Standing-pilot gas furnaces represent a significant number of residential gas furnaces that are still in use today. A standing-pilot gas furnace is equipped with a naturally aspirating gas burner, a draft hood, a solenoid-operated main gas valve, a continuously operating pilot light (standing-pilot), a thermocouple safety device, a 24-volt AC transformer, a heat exchanger, a blower and motor assembly, and one or more air filters. The standing-pilot is the main distinguishing characteristic of the low-efficiency conventional gas furnace.

## Mid-Efficiency

A mid-efficiency gas furnace is equipped with a naturally aspirating gas burner and a pilot light. The pilot light is unlike a standing-pilot. It does not run continuously. The pilot light is shut off when the furnace is not in operation — when the thermostat is not calling for heat. The heat exchanger is more efficient than one inside a conventional furnace. There's no draft hood. There may be a small fan installed in the flue pipe to create an induced draft, so these furnaces are sometimes referred to as induced-draft furnaces. A mid-efficiency gas furnace is also equipped with automatic controls, blower and motor assembly, venting, and air filtering. Some mid-efficiency furnaces have a motorized damper installed in the exhaust flue pipe. A mid-efficiency furnace is about 20% more energy-efficient than a conventional gas furnace. A mid-efficiency furnace has an AFUE rating of 78 to 82%. The intermittent pilot is the main distinguishing characteristic.

## High-Efficiency

CONDENSATION IN A HIGH-EFFICIENCY FURNACE

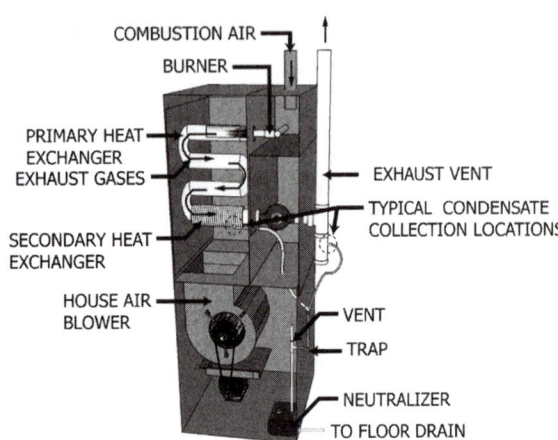

High-efficiency gas furnaces have AFUE ratings of 90% and greater. A solid-state control board controls the ignition. There is no continuous pilot light. There are two or sometimes three heat exchangers installed inside a high-efficiency gas furnace. Condensate is produced when heat is extracted from the flue gases. The temperature of the flue gases is low enough to use a PVC pipe as the vent exhaust pipe. There is no need to vent the exhaust gases up a chimney stack.

There are two different types of high-efficiency furnaces: one with an intermittent pilot or direct spark; and one with a hot-surface ignition system. The production of excessive condensate is the main distinguishing characteristic.

## Intermittent Pilot Furnace

When the thermostat on a furnace that has an intermittent pilot calls for heat, there is a short ignition period when a high-voltage spark is generated. The spark ignites the pilot.

When lighting the pilot flame, the flame must be confirmed through a flame-confirmation process. If the flame is confirmed, a control module sends a signal to the main gas valve. The valve opens. The gas flows to the burner. The pilot flame lights the gas burner. The burners continue to burn until the thermostat is satisfied at a desired temperature. The satisfied thermostat signals to stop the ignition process and shuts off the pilot and burner.

## Hot-Surface Ignition (HSI) Furnace

The hot-surface ignition furnace typically has two or more heat exchangers. There's no pilot light. Instead, there is an electric ignition device. This device is often called a glow plug or glow stick. The HSI starts the gas burner. When the thermostat calls for heat, a purge cycle starts with the draft fan activating. Then the igniter lights up to a very high (hot) temperature. The gas valve is opened, and gas flows to the burner and is ignited by the HSI. A sensor confirms that there is a gas flame at the burner nozzle, and then the electric power to the igniter is turned off.

INTERMITTENT PILOT LIGHT

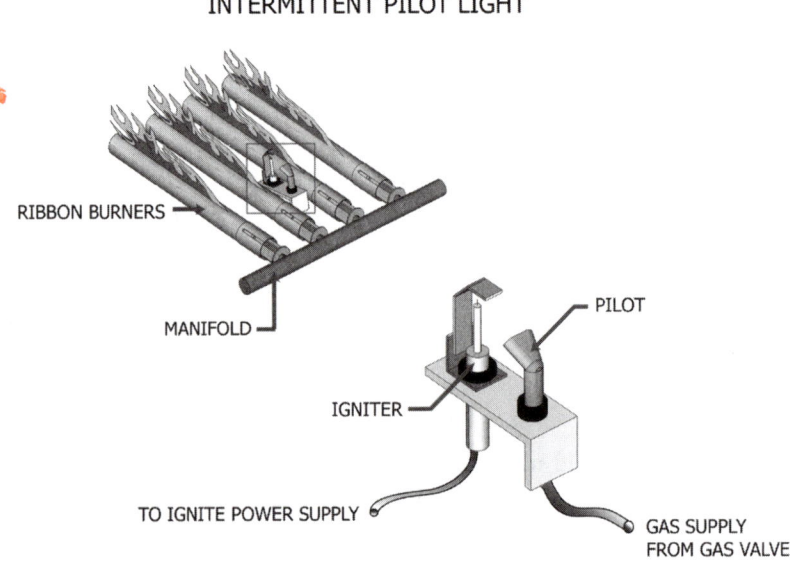

## Gas Furnace Components

Most forced warm-air furnaces have the following components and controls:

- thermostat;
- furnace controls;
- heat exchanger;
- gas burners;
- ignition system;
- blower fan; and
- air filter.

SAFETY DEVICES FOR A HIGH EFFICIENCY FURNACE

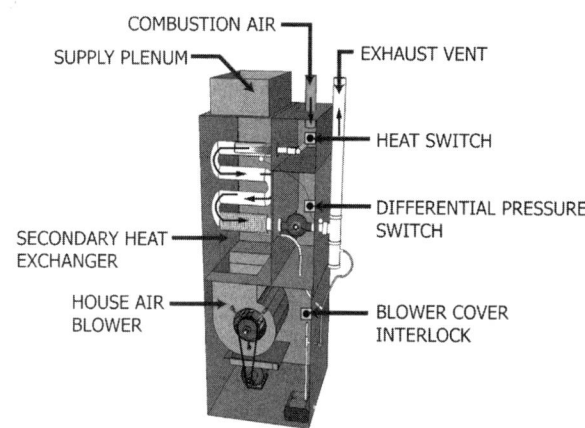

## Furnace Controls

The following is a list of some of the furnace controls that may be found at a gas furnace:

- thermostat;
- main gas valve;
- thermocouple;
- thermopile;
- mercury flame sensor;
- gas-pressure regulator;
- fan and limit control;
- heat exchanger;
- gas burners;
- blower fan and motor; and
- air filtering.

FAN/LIMIT SWITCH

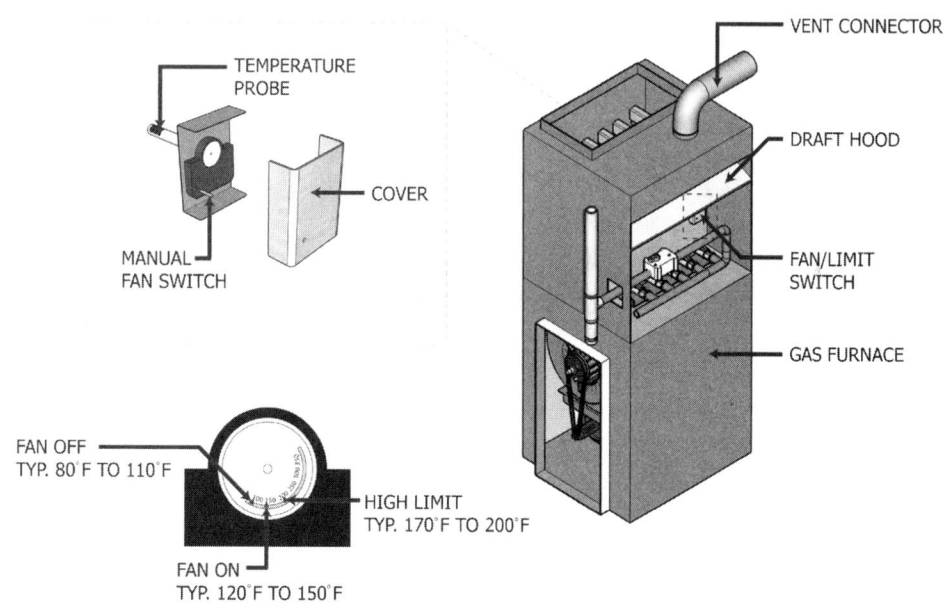

## Thermostat

A thermostat controls the operation of the furnace. The thermostat senses the air temperature in the room or space that is being heated. It sends signals to open and close the main gas valve.

## Heat Exchanger

The heat exchanger is a metal surface located in between the hot combustion gases and the air that is circulating through the furnace. The hot combustion gases heat up the metal material of the heat exchanger, and the heat is transferred from the hot metal to the air passing through it. The warm air is forced through the ducts or pipes by a blower fan and distributed to the rooms or areas of the building.

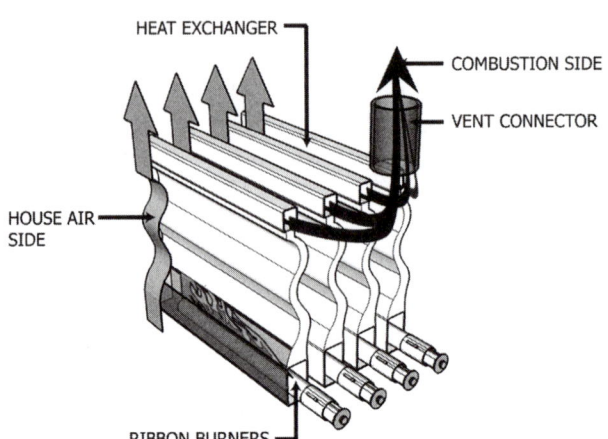

HEAT EXCHANGER HEAT FLOW

HEAT EXCHANGER

COMBUSTION SIDE

VENT CONNECTOR

HOUSE AIR SIDE

RIBBON BURNERS

## Thermocouple

A thermocouple is a device that senses heat. It's used in gas furnaces having a standing pilot light. It determines whether the pilot flame is lit before the main gas valve is opened to supply gas to the burners. The flame must be lit before the valve is opened.

The heat of the pilot flame is converted to electricity by the thermocouple. It turns heat into an electrical current. The current is strong enough to open the main gas valve. After being opened, the gas flows to the pilot light. If the thermocouple does not detect a pilot flame, it will turn off the gas supply to the pilot. The electrical current from a 24-volt AC transformer operates the main gas valve.

## Thermopile

Instead of a thermocouple, a thermopile is used in some standing-pilot gas furnaces. A thermopile senses the heat from a pilot-light flame. It is larger than a thermocouple. It operates both the main gas valve and the pilot light. If there is a thermopile present, there's no transformer required.

## Mercury Flame Sensor

A mercury flame sensor may be used in an electronic ignition system. It consists of a sensor filled with mercury, a capillary tube, and a switch. The burner flame heats up the sensor.

## Gas-Pressure Regulator

The pressure regulator is installed on the main gas valve. It regulates the gas pressure, ensuring a constant gas pressure in the burner manifold. In a propane gas heating system, the regulator is located between the supply tank and the main gas valve.

## Fan and Limit Control

The fan and limit control is a safety device. It is installed inside the furnace plenum where it senses the air temperature that passes through that area. It controls the operation of the furnace within a temperature range, usually between 80° F and 150° F. It prevents the furnace from overheating by turning off the gas supply to the burner assembly. It can also turn off the fan when the burner has been turned off and the temperature drops below the lowest setting.

## Heat Exchanger

The heat exchanger is made of steel. It may be aluminum or galvanized. In hostile environments, heat exchangers can be coated with a porcelain material to provide protection against corrosive chemicals.

The flames come from the burner and go into an enclosure called a combustion chamber or firebox. The heat exchanger is located directly above that. The heat from the combustion process taking place is transferred to the metal walls of the heat exchanger. The heat is transferred from the metal to the air that passes through the exchanger.

The heat exchanger can reach several hundred degrees in temperature. Air flowing across the heat exchanger must travel at a high speed and must be uniform across all sections of the exchanger. If the air flow is low across one section, that section of the exchanger will overheat and may cause a failure in the exchanger.

There are sections of the heat exchanger called cells. There's one cell for each burner, and the burner is located directly below the exchanger cell. The heat moves up from the burner through the cell. At the top of the heat exchanger, a manifold combines all of the open cells into one collection device. The manifold collects the exhaust gases coming up and out of each cell and directs the gases into the exhaust outlet. The vent connector pipe (or metal flue pipe) is connected to the outlet. The exhaust gases vent through this pipe to the outside.

The exhaust gases heat up the exchanger to a very high temperature. Air from the house's interior passes up through the exchanger, and heat is transferred. Air enters the exchanger at about 70° F and exits at about 140° F. A temperature rise of about 70° F to 110° F is acceptable.

Overheating and failure at a section of the heat exchanger may be caused by a flame touching the inner surface of the heat exchanger's metal. Under normal conditions, the flame should not touch the heat exchanger.

Overheating and failure at a section of the heat exchanger may also be caused by excessive firing of the burners, called over-firing.

The heat exchanger should not be covered with soot, carbon deposits, or other debris. That will reduce the furnace's efficiency. Dirty heat exchangers should be cleaned by a qualified technician.

## Gas Burners

There are two broad categories of burners. One is mono-port; the other is multi-port. You will find mono-port burners installed in a furnace with a forced draft, rather than a natural draft. Mono-port burners are common with high-efficiency furnaces. They can fire and operate in any direction or

### GAS SUPPLY TO BURNERS

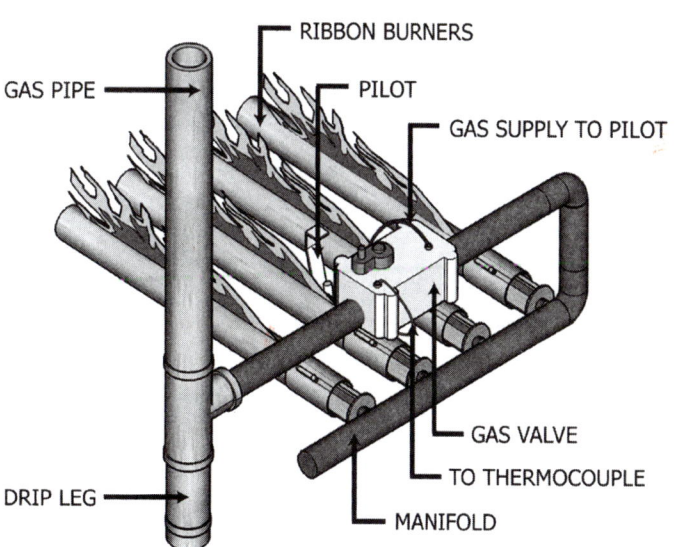

RIBBON BURNERS
PILOT
GAS SUPPLY TO PILOT
GAS PIPE
GAS VALVE
TO THERMOCOUPLE
MANIFOLD
DRIP LEG

orientation. Upflow, downflow and horizontal furnaces can use mono-ports.

Multi-port burners are generally found on conventional furnaces. Multi-port burners can be ribbon, drilled, or slotted burners.

## Primary and Secondary Air

Gas burners combine the proper mixture of air and gas for the combustion process. Both primary and secondary air are required. Primary air is that which mixes with the gas before going to the burners. Secondary air is that which is added to the flame for proper combustion. Secondary air flows around the burners and heat exchanger. It mixes with unburned gas in the heat exchanger. Secondary air is drawn into the burner by a draft.

## Crossover Igniter

Many gas furnaces have individual chambers or sections of the heat exchanger. Inside each section is a flame burner. To prevent unburned gas from entering the combustion chamber, all burners should fire up at almost the same time.

This simultaneous ignition can be provided by a gas burner component called a crossover burner or crossover igniter. The crossover igniter is installed perpendicular to and across the top of all of the main burners, connecting them all together. When one burner ignites, the crossover carries a flame to the other burners and ignites them. It bridges the flame from one burner to the next.

## Flames

If you are looking at the flames of a burner, the flame's color should appear blue. The flame should be stable and not waving. It should not lift off the burner. It should not float around the sides of the burner or drift out. Yellow tips on the flames may mean that there's inadequate primary air. A waving flame may indicate a venting or draft problem. It could also mean a crack in the heat exchanger. You do not want to see the flames roll out of the combustion chamber when the gas ignites. This could indicate a problem with the firing, a block in the venting, or inadequate secondary air. Look for scorched metal or damaged wiring in the front of the unit.

### CROSSOVER IGNITERS

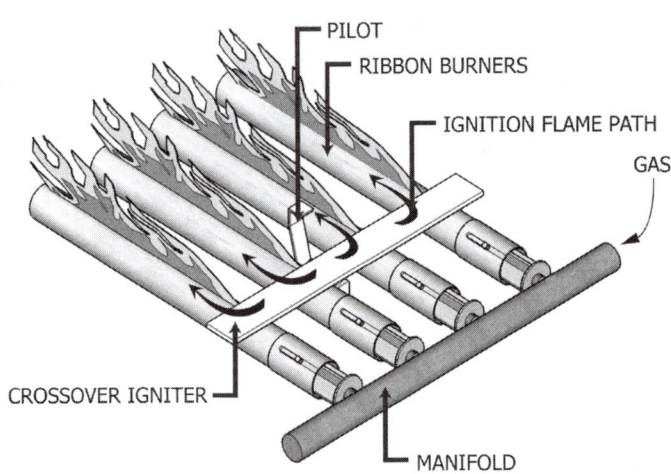

- PILOT
- RIBBON BURNERS
- IGNITION FLAME PATH
- GAS
- CROSSOVER IGNITER
- MANIFOLD

**Inspection Tip:** After the burners on a conventional furnace ignite, look at the flames. Watch the flames while the blower fan turns on. If the flames waver at that particular moment, it might indicate a cracked heat exchanger.

## Blower Fan and Motor

Forced warm-air furnaces have blower fans installed. A blower fan has two functions:

- it moves heated air through the distribution supply ducts or pipes; and

• it protects the heat exchanger from overheating by blowing air across its metal surfaces.

The air enters the furnace, gets heated, and is circulated throughout the building. Some say that the fan draws in (or sucks) the air into the furnace. Others say that it blows air out through the system. Whichever is the case, the primary function of the blower fan is air circulation.

The fan motors are either belt-driven or direct-drive. Most modern furnaces have blower fans with direct-drive motors. Direct-drive motors have various fan speeds than can be set and adjusted by wiring. Belt-driven motors can be adjusted for various speeds by physically adjusting the distance between the fixed flange and the movable pulley.

Modern blower fans have multiple speeds. A multi-speed fan operates at a low speed when the furnace is off. This allows the air to move slowly and helps with air filtration and humidification, for example. The blower fan operates at a high speed when the furnace is operating or when the air-conditioning system is turned on. When the air-conditioning system is on, the blower fan automatically turns on at a higher speed.

## Rust

There are many reasons that rust may accumulate on the burners, including:

- a condensate or water leak from above;
- condensation in the flue running back into the combustion chamber; or
- a clothes dryer venting into the furnace room.

## Dirt and Soot

Dirt and soot on the burners could cause incomplete combustion and make the furnace work harder to heat the house. Dirty burners likely indicate delayed maintenance.

## Air Filtering

All forced warm-air heating systems should have air filtering installed. There is a variety of air filters available for furnaces. Many furnaces are equipped with a disposable air filter that cleans the circulating air. There are also washable air filters, and electronic air filters. Electronic filters are high-efficiency air filters.

Air filters should be installed in the path of the air that enters the heating system, in the return plenum or duct.

Proper maintenance of the air filter is important for the efficiency of the furnace. A dirty or clogged air filter restricts the air flow through the system and can cause an excessive rise in the temperature. This temperature rise can decrease the furnace's operating efficiency and may even cause damage to the heat exchanger.

A disposable air filter should be checked every month and replaced when dirty. If a permanent air filter is installed, it should be checked and cleaned periodically according to the manufacturer's recommendation.

## Venting

There are six basic ways to vent the combustion products to the outside. They are:

- masonry chimneys;
- low-heat Type A chimneys;
- Type B gas vents;
- Type C gas vents;
- wall venting; and
- PVC pipe venting.

## Masonry Chimneys

Masonry chimneys should have a flue that is lined. Smooth tile is one common material for flue liners. Many chimneys are made of metal. They can be prefabricated, and they should be listed by the Underwriters Laboratories for use with fuel-burning appliances.

If an old, conventional low-efficiency furnace has been replaced by a mid-efficiency or high-efficiency furnace, the masonry chimney may not be suitable for use any longer. The gases that come out of the more efficient system are much cooler than those that are produced by a standing-pilot gas furnace. The cool gases are not buoyant enough to rise through the chimney. They will condense inside the chimney flue and will damage the masonry.

A chimney provides a draft and a means to vent the combustion byproducts of the furnace. A good chimney draft is not necessary for the combustion process in a furnace, but it is essential for venting the combustion byproducts to the outside through the chimney.

The height of a typical masonry chimney should be at least 3 feet above the roof surface, or 2 feet higher than any other part of the building within 10 feet of the chimney.

## Type A Chimneys

Type A chimneys are low-heat, prefabricated metal chimneys. They have been tested and approved by the Underwriters Laboratories.

## Type B Gas Vents

Type B gas vents are UL-listed. They are recommended for all standard gas-fired heating systems with draft hoods and other Category I appliances.

## Type BW Vents

Type BW vents are for wall furnaces.

## Type C Gas Vents

Type C gas vents are typically used for standard gas-fired furnaces that are installed in the attic space.

## Type L Vents

Type L vents are for appliances listed for use with Type L or Type B vents.

## Wall Venting

Wall venting involves having the combustion, combustion air, and combustion byproducts venting all separated from the interior air of the room or space being heated. The combustion gases are vented through the wall.

## PVC Pipe Venting

High-efficiency furnaces use PVC piping to vent combustion gases and byproducts outside. You usually see the PVC pipe extending from the furnace through the wall to the outside. A PVC vent pipe will likely indicate a high-efficiency gas heating system. The pipe is typically 2 inches in diameter. PVC is also used to bring fresh outdoor air into the system for combustion. It could be very long — sometimes as long as 60 feet.

The temperatures of the combustion byproducts are low—100° F to 150° F. That's very cool. The PVC does not melt. It will feel warm to the touch. That's one way to determine which pipe is the exhaust.

High-efficiency furnaces should not be vented into a chimney. The exhaust gases from a high-efficiency heating system are too cool to create enough chimney draft. The cool gases will condense inside the chimney and cause damage.

PVC pipes need a proper slope. The pipe should be sloped down and toward the furnace, or slope up and away from the furnace. Typically, ¼-inch per linear foot is recommended. The pipe should be sloped and adequately supported so that condensate does not form and puddle inside a sagging part of the vent pipe. The condensate should be allowed to drain back toward the furnace.

## Flue Pipe

### CHIMNEY/VENT CONNECTIONS

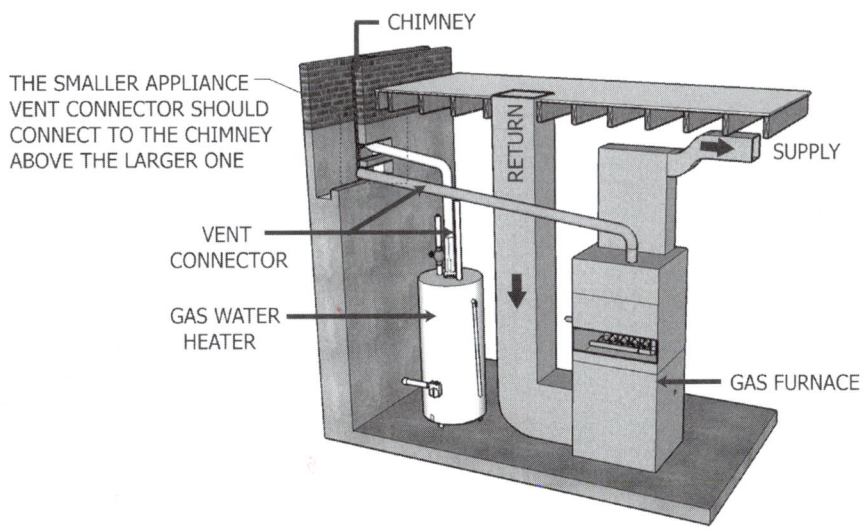

THE SMALLER APPLIANCE VENT CONNECTOR SHOULD CONNECT TO THE CHIMNEY ABOVE THE LARGER ONE

CHIMNEY

RETURN

SUPPLY

VENT CONNECTOR

GAS WATER HEATER

GAS FURNACE

The flue is the passage through which the gases from the combustion chamber of the heating system move to the outside. A flue is also referred to as the flue pipe, vent pipe, or vent connector. A chimney flue is the flue that is inside a chimney.

The flue from the heating system to the chimney is often called the vent connector, chimney connector, or smoke pipe. A flue outlet, or vent, is the opening in a heating system through which the flue gases move.

## Flue Details

The flue pipe (or vent pipe or vent connector) connects the outlet of the heating system to the chimney. The flue pipe should not extend farther than the inner liner surface of the chimney flue.

The flue pipe of a heating system (furnace or boiler) should not be sharing the same chimney as a conventional fireplace. Flue pipes from two appliances should not enter a chimney from opposite sides at the same height. From the point where a flue pipe enters the chimney stack, there should be at least 2 feet of clearance above the chimney cleanout.

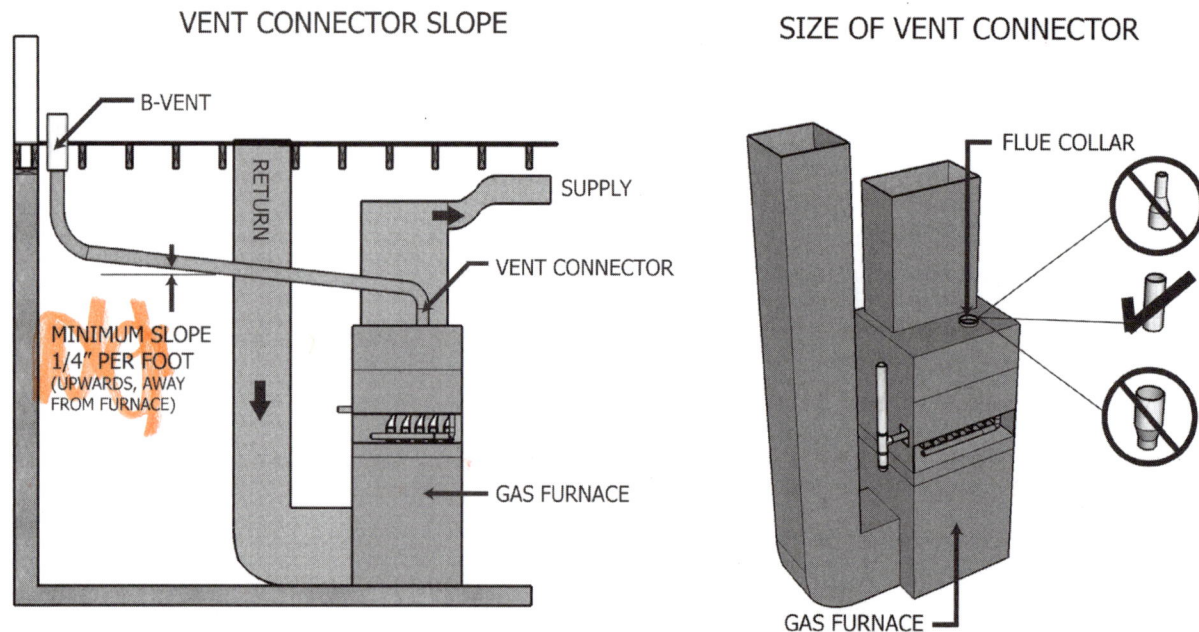

VENT CONNECTOR SLOPE

SIZE OF VENT CONNECTOR

The flue pipe should have a slope of ¼-inch per linear foot. The flue pipe's horizontal run should not exceed 75% of the vertical run. The vent pipe crossovers in an attic should extend at an angle that is at least 60 degrees from the vertical.

The flue pipe should be at least the same diameter size as the outlet of the furnace. The diameter size of the flue pipe should never be reduced.

## Draft Hood

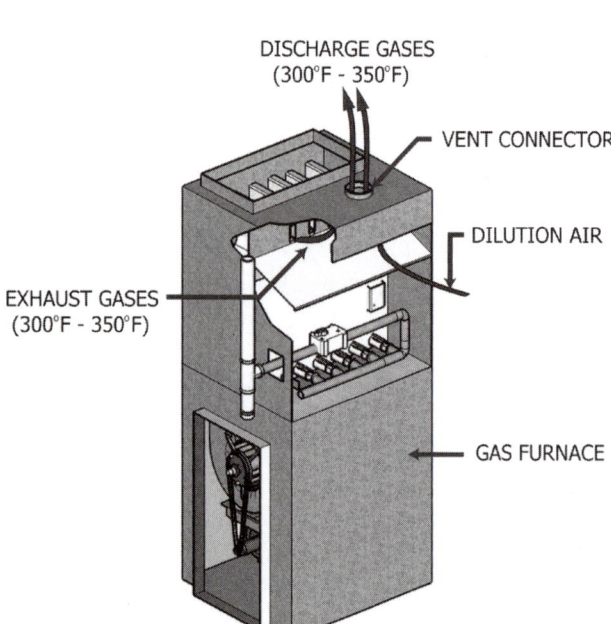

INTERNAL DRAFT DIVERTER

A draft hood is installed on standing-pilot gas furnaces. Mid- and high-efficiency gas furnaces do not have draft hoods. Draft hoods are attached to the top of the furnace above the flue outlet. It is sometimes called a draft diverter.

The draft hood functions to produce a constant low draft of air for the combustion chamber. It allows dilution air to be drawn into the vent pipe. The dilution air cools the exhaust and ensures a good draft. The draft hood also prevents large downdrafts from the chimney affecting the burner.

The draft hood can be built into the furnace cabinet (internal draft diverter), or it could be installed separately above the top of the heating unit. If it is installed within the furnace cabinet, it becomes part of the manifold that collects all of the exhaust gases that come out of each cell of the exchanger.

## Heat Shield

Most conventional gas furnaces have a heat shield. This prevents flame rollout. It contains the flames inside the burner chamber. It also protects the burners against strong drafts.

## Gas Supply Piping

The gas supply piping is sometimes referred to as the gas service piping. The gas piping must be installed properly according to the local codes and ordinances, or, if unavailable, the codes in established standards, such as the National Fuel Gas Code. The codes will recommend the proper sizing of the pipes for the required gas volumes.

The inlet gas supply pipe should be at least ½-inch. The gas line from the supply should serve only a single heating system. There should be a drip leg installed near the heating system.

DRAFT DIVERTER ON VENT CONNECTOR

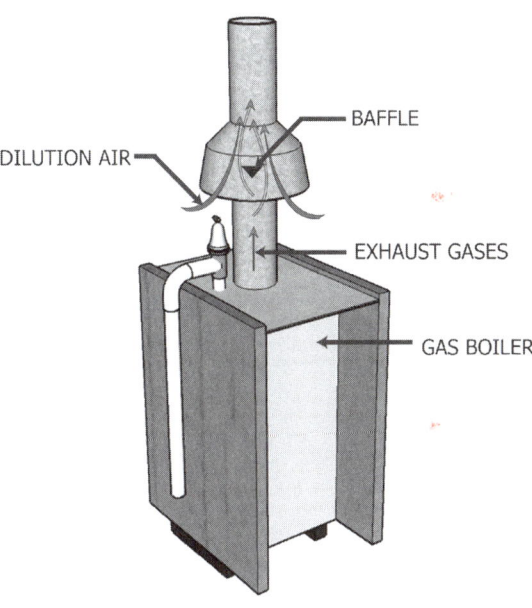

A drip leg should be installed at the bottom of the gas supply riser near the heating system. The drip leg collects dirt, moisture and impurities that float in the gas.

A gas shut-off valve should be installed near the heating system. This manual shut-off valve is sometimes installed on the gas-supply riser, or on the horizontal pipe between the riser and the union fitting near the heating system.

The union-joint fitting should be installed between the manual shut-off valve and the main gas control valve on the heating system. The union joint allows the gas burner assembly to be easily disconnected for service.

## Gas Furnace Inspection, Service and Maintenance

The heating system should be inspected by a qualified service technician every year. It is recommended that the system be inspected before the heating season. The technician can ensure the continued safe operation of the heating system.

# Quiz #6

1. A _____ is approximately the amount of energy needed to heat 1 pound of water by 1° F.

☑ BTU

☐ gas-foot-pound

☐ steady-state

2. Older gas furnaces have a(n) _____ pilot light that is always burning.

☑ standing

☐ direct-spark

☐ intermittent

3. T/F: There may be at least two heat exchangers inside a high-efficiency furnace.

☑ True

☐ False

4. _____ air is air that mixes with the gas before going to the burners.

☐ Secondary

☑ Primary

☐ Crossover

**Answer Key is on page 118.**

# Oil Furnaces

There are different types of oil furnaces according to their orientation. They can be described as:

- upflow;
- downflow (or counterflow); or
- horizontal-flow.

They can be of various capacities, sizes and efficiencies. They can be installed in various spaces, including basements, attics and closets. All furnaces should be UL-listed and tested for safety.

## Conventional Oil Furnace

Most residential oil furnaces in homes today are conventional. They are not high-efficiency condensing heating systems. These conventional furnaces are slowly being replaced by mid- and high-efficiency heating systems. If you are inspecting a conventional oil furnace with a cast-iron burner, it likely has an AFUE (seasonal efficiency rating) of 60%, which is categorized as low-efficiency.

## Heating Cycle

Let's go over the general steps of the heating cycle for a conventional oil furnace. First, the thermostat calls for heat. The thermostat closes an electrical circuit to a control relay. Electrical current is sent to both the oil burner transformer and the fuel pump motor.

The motor on the fuel pump sucks fuel oil from the supply tank and pushes it to the burner nozzle of the gun assembly. At the burner nozzle, fuel is combined with air. The fuel is atomized. A blower sends combustion air into the combustion chamber. The transformer sends a high-voltage electric current to the electrodes in the gun assembly. The atomized air-fuel mixture is ignited. A rumbling sound is created by this burner. This noise signals that the heating cycle has begun.

There is a safety device in operation when the burner is shooting flames. It is a cadmium sulfide photo-cell, referred to as a cad cell. The cad cell "looks" for a flame and confirms that it exists. It can detect the flame located in the combustion chamber. If the cad cell doesn't see the flame within a few seconds, the circuit to the burner is opened and the burner is shut down.

Some oil furnaces don't have a cad cell and instead have a stack relay. A stack relay senses heat instead of light. If the stack relay does not sense heat, the circuit to the burner is opened and the burner is shut down.

This safety device in an oil furnace is similar to the function of the fan and limit control for a gas furnace.

## Mid-Efficiency and High-Efficiency Oil Furnaces

The energy efficiency of an oil furnace is measured by its annual fuel utilization efficiency rating, or AFUE. The higher the AFUE number, the higher the efficiency. The minimum rating for furnaces is 78%. Mid-efficiency furnaces have a rating range of 78 to 82%. High-efficiency furnaces have a rating range of 88 to 92%. Older conventional furnaces have a rating of around 60 to 65%.

## Mid-Efficiency (Non-Condensing)

A typical non-condensing, mid-efficiency oil furnace uses less oil than a conventional furnace. At a mid-efficiency, non-condensing unit, a burner shoots flames and heat into a combustion chamber. The chamber (or firepot) is usually made of some type of heat-resistant ceramic material. Combustion air is drawn into the burner assembly by a fan, where it mixes with the oil. The gun ignites the oil-air mixture. Flames shoot into the chamber, and heat passes up through the heat exchanger. The combustion byproducts are vented to the outside. The blower fan pushes air through the furnace across the heat exchanger. Heat is transferred from the metal of the exchanger to the air. Many mid-efficiency furnaces do not use a chimney to vent the combustion byproducts outside but simply vent through a sidewall of the building. A draft damper (or barometric damper) is not necessary on the flue pipe.

## High-Efficiency (Condensing)

A typical high-efficiency condensing furnace has two heat exchangers. The heat exchangers are designed to extract most of the heat from the combustion gases before they are vented outside. The second heat exchanger extracts the latent heat that is in the water vapor of the combustion gases. Extracting the heat lowers the temperature. The lower temperature causes condensate to form. The extracted heat is added to the warm air being circulated. The condensate drains from the heating system. The cool combustion gases are vented outside through a PVC vent pipe installed through the sidewall of the building.

## Components of an Oil Furnace

The main components of an oil-fired, warm-air heating system include the:

- furnace controls;
- heat exchanger;
- burner assembly;
- fuel pump and motor;
- blower and motor;
- combustion blower;
- cleanout and observation port;
- vent opening; and
- air filtering.

## Furnace Controls

The furnace controls for a typical oil furnace include the:

- thermostat;
- cad cell;
- fan controls; and
- delayed-action solenoid valve.

The **thermostat** controls the operation of the heating system. It senses the air temperature in the room that is being heated. It calls for heat.

The **cad cell** is a safety device. It "looks" for the flame inside the burner chamber. It confirms that a flame exists when the burner starts. If the cad cell doesn't see the flame within a few seconds, the circuit to the burner is opened and the burner is shut down.

The **fan and limit control** is a safety device. It is installed in a metal box on the outside of the oil furnace. It senses the air temperature that passes through the furnace plenum. It is located on the house-air side of the heat exchanger, and it measures the temperature of the air that is coming out of the heat exchanger. It controls the operation of the blower fan within a temperature range. It prevents the furnace from overheating by turning off the burner if the furnace gets too hot.

When the air coming out of the furnace's heat exchanger is warm enough, it turns on the blower fan and pushes air to the rooms and spaces of the building being heated.

The fan and limit control has two settings: high and low. When the temperature in the house reaches the upper setting, the burner turns off. The blower fan runs until the temperature of the heat exchanger lowers and reaches the low setting, and then the blower fan turns off.

The control is usually set to turn the blower fan on when the air temperature reaches around 120° F to 150° F. That same sensor control also turns the fan off when the air temperature drops to around 80° F to 110° F.

Some modern oil furnaces are equipped with electronic devices that control the blower fan instead of the fan and limit-control switches.

## Heat Exchanger for an Oil Furnace

The heat exchanger is the part of the furnace that transfers heat energy from the material of the exchanger to the air that passes through the furnace and around the exchanger.

The exchanger is made of heavy-gauge steel. The exchanger has an upper and a lower chamber. The lower part contains the combustion chamber, where the flames are.

## Combustion Chamber (Firepot)

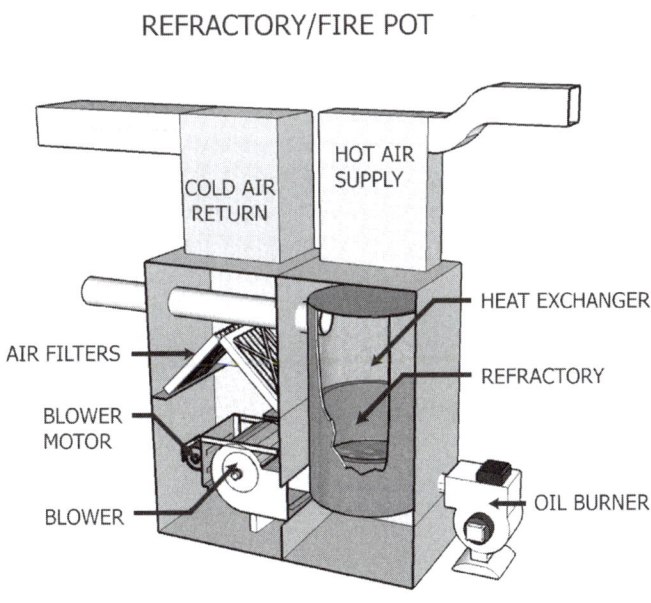

REFRACTORY/FIRE POT

COLD AIR RETURN

HOT AIR SUPPLY

HEAT EXCHANGER

REFRACTORY

AIR FILTERS

BLOWER MOTOR

BLOWER

OIL BURNER

The combustion chamber (often referred to as the firepot) is where the combustion takes place. The combustion chamber is inside the lower part of the heat exchanger. The combustion chamber is made of a material that can withstand very high temperatures. Combustion chambers can be made of stainless steel, cast iron, or a refractory material, such as firebrick or ceramic clay. The nozzle of the burner-gun assembly sticks into the chamber area. Most chambers are round, but some are square or octagonal. Some modern oil furnaces have sealed combustion chambers that help to increase their efficiency.

Combustion chambers are typically about 10 inches in diameter (or wide) and 13 inches tall.

## Oil Burners

The most common oil burner that you will see is the atomizing oil burner, sometimes called a gun-type burner. There are some special burners called vaporizing or pot-type burners. There are a few parts to an atomizing oil-burner assembly that are important, including the:

- burner control;
- re-set button;
- oil pump;
- ignition transformer;
- cad cell;
- gun;
- nozzle; and
- electrodes.

An atomizing burner uses an electric pump and a nozzle that atomizes the oil. "Atomizing" means that the oil is turned from a liquid to a spray of fine droplets. This spray is mixed with air. The mixture is then ignited by a high-voltage spark.

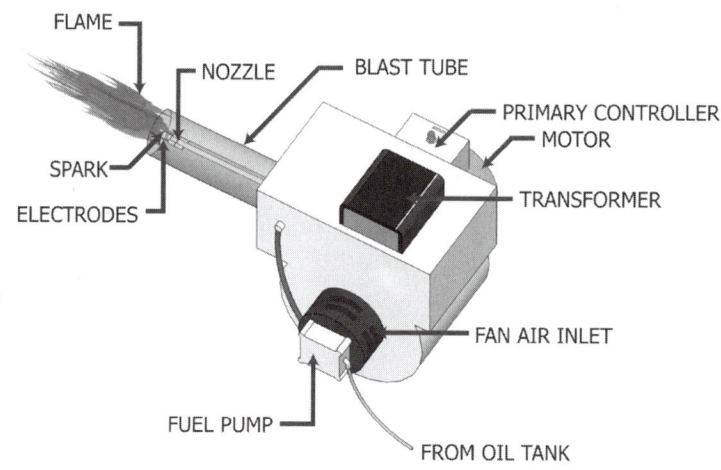

ATOMIZING OIL BURNER

FLAME · NOZZLE · BLAST TUBE · PRIMARY CONTROLLER · MOTOR · TRANSFORMER · SPARK · ELECTRODES · FAN AIR INLET · FUEL PUMP · FROM OIL TANK

The burner combines the fuel oil with air and mixes them together. It delivers the fuel-air mixture to the gun and ignites it.

The oil pump on the oil burner sucks oil from the oil storage tank and sends it to the gun. The pump delivers the oil under pressure (around 75 to 120 psi). The pump is usually mounted on the side of the burner assembly.

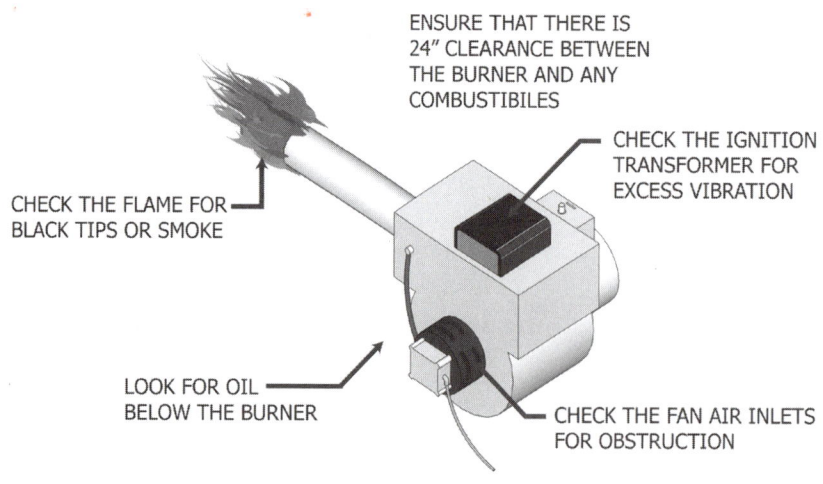

INSPECTING AN OIL BURNER

ENSURE THAT THERE IS 24" CLEARANCE BETWEEN THE BURNER AND ANY COMBUSTIBILES

CHECK THE IGNITION TRANSFORMER FOR EXCESS VIBRATION

CHECK THE FLAME FOR BLACK TIPS OR SMOKE

LOOK FOR OIL BELOW THE BURNER

CHECK THE FAN AIR INLETS FOR OBSTRUCTION

LISTEN FOR EXCESS OR UNUSUAL NOISE FROM THE BURNER

Air for combustion is sucked into the burner by a combustion-air fan. Air gets sucked through the air ports and is forced down the blast tube of the gun and into the head, where the electrodes are located. The barrel of the gun is a steel tube about 3 inches in diameter and about 1 foot long. The electrodes are at the end of the tube.

On modern burners, the flame-retention burner device is usually located at the very end of the tube.

OIL BURNER WITH FLAME RETENTION HEAD

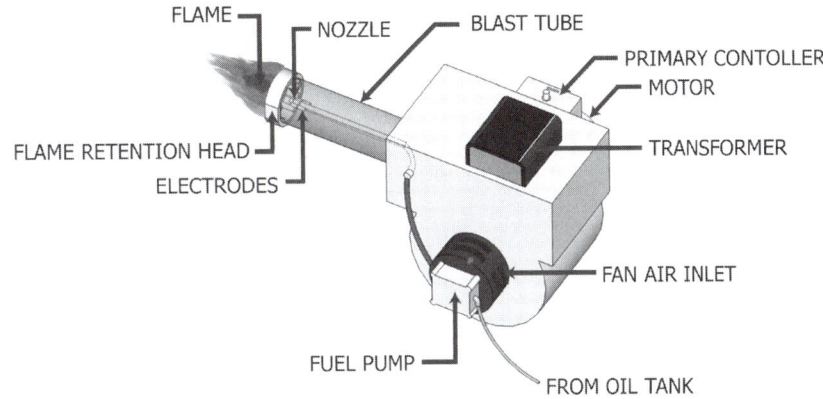

### Electrodes

The electrodes behave like a big spark plug. The electrodes create a high-voltage spark, and the spark ignites the oil spray. Once the flame is confirmed, the spark shuts off and the flame continues to burn.

The combustion is contained inside the firepot or refractor chamber pot.

### Ignition Transformer

The ignition transformer takes the 120-volt electric current and changes it into a very high DC voltage for the electrodes to create a spark.

### Oil Burner Flame

Most burners have a flame that looks like a blowtorch with a long ragged flame. The flame is usually orange and yellow, with yellow tips. There may be some gray or black smoke above the flame. Modern burners may have a blue color at the flame's core, and a tight, rounded flame pattern.

### Blower Circulating Fan

The main blower circulating fan circulates air through the furnace and pushes the heated air through the distribution ducts or pipes and into the various rooms and spaces of the building. The fan draws cool air into the furnace and pushes the air around the heat exchanger, where the heat is transferred from the exchanger to the air. Both belt-drive and direct-drive blowers can be found on oil furnaces. Newer furnaces may have blowers with variable speeds.

### Combustion-Air Blower Fans

Some high-efficiency oil furnaces are equipped with little blower fans that supply air into the combustion chamber.

## Observation Ports

Some oil furnaces have one or more observation ports (or cleanout ports) that can be used for observation and also for cleaning the heat exchanger and chamber area.

## Air Filtering

All forced warm-air heating systems should have air filtering installed. There are many types of air filters available for furnaces. Many furnaces are equipped with a disposable air filter that cleans the circulating air. There are washable air filters and high-efficiency electronic air filters.

Air filters should be installed in the path of the air that enters the heating system in the cool-air return plenum or duct.

Proper maintenance of the air filter is important for the efficiency of the furnace. A dirty or clogged air filter restricts the air flow through the system and can cause an excessive rise in the temperature. This temperature rise may cause damage to the heat exchanger or lower its operating efficiency.

A disposable air filter should be checked every month and replaced when dirty. If a permanent air filter is installed, it should be checked and cleaned periodically, according to the manufacturer's recommendation.

## Venting

Generally speaking, oil furnaces vent in the same way that gas furnaces do. High-efficiency oil furnaces can use PVC piping to vent the combustion byproducts and gases to the outside through a sidewall of the building.

## Flue Pipe

A metal flue pipe may be installed at the oil furnace. There should be a slope to the horizontal run of the flue pipe of at least ¼-inch per linear foot. Ideally, the furnace should not be more than 10 flue-pipe diameters from the chimney connection. Appropriate clearances must be maintained from the hot flue pipe to combustible materials.

## Barometric Damper

EXTERIOR ABOVE GROUND OIL STORAGE TANK

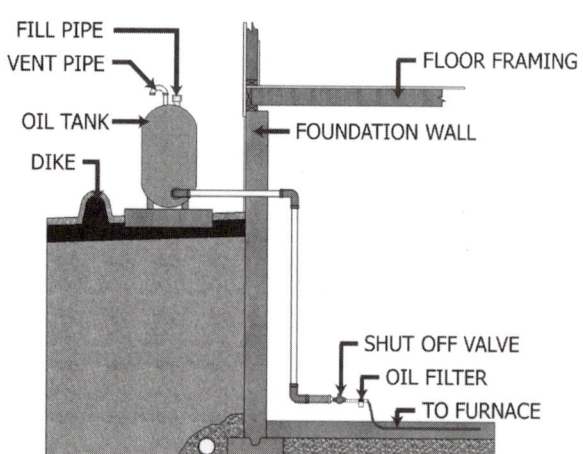

A barometric damper is often called the draft regulator or barometric draft regulator. The barometric damper provides the proper draft in the oil furnace by automatically reducing or diluting the chimney draft to the optimal amount. The barometric damper on an oil furnace is similar to that of the draft hood on a gas-fired appliance. Dampers or regulators are recommended for all oil furnaces (or oil-fired appliances) that are connected to a chimney, unless the particular unit is listed for use without one.

When inspecting, you should find the damper in the horizontal flue pipe located as close as possible to the chimney.

## Oil Fuel Supply Tank

The fuel supply tank is often called the oil storage tank. The fuel supply tank holds the fuel oil. It can be located inside or outside. It could be located above or below the level of the heating system. If the tank is located outside, it could be underground or above ground.

A tank may be made of fiberglass, but it's typically made of 14-gauge steel. The typical capacity of an oil tank is 275 gallons.

The tank is directly connected to the fuel pump of the heating system with a fuel line.

There are one-pipe systems and two-pipe systems that connect the tank to the heating system. When you see a one-pipe system where only one fuel line pipe is connected to the burner assembly, the tank is usually installed in the same location as the heating system, such as both being located in the basement. When you see a two-pipe system where there are two fuel line pipes, then the tank is usually located outside. The distance between the tank and the heating system is likely long, with the tank located vertically above the heating system; otherwise, the tank cannot use gravity to move the oil to the burner.

A shut-off valve should be installed on the suction line. You may find a valve installed near the tank or near the heating system.

In general, the filler pipe should be a minimum of 2 inches in diameter, and the vent pipe 1¼ inches in diameter. The pipes should be made of wrought iron. The oil supply lines between the oil supply tank and the oil burner should be made of copper tubing.

## Oil Filter

An oil filter should be installed on the fuel line in between the oil storage tank and the burner. The oil filter will likely be a cartridge-type. The filter cartridge should be changed at least once a year. The filter body should be cleaned before a new cartridge is installed.

The filter prevents sludge in the oil from clogging the fuel pump and the oil burner nozzle, which otherwise will cause system failure.

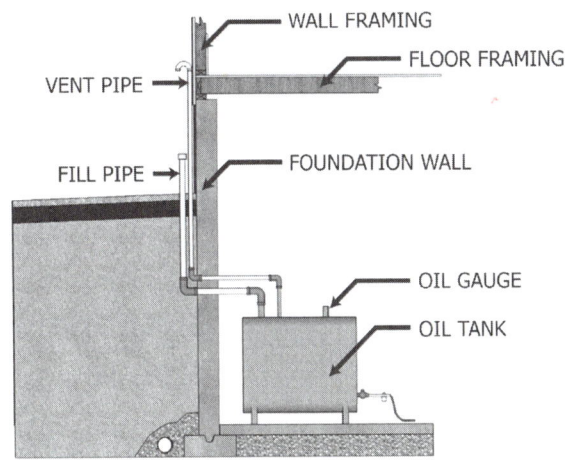

FILL AND VENT PIPING

WALL FRAMING

FLOOR FRAMING

VENT PIPE

FOUNDATION WALL

FILL PIPE

OIL GAUGE

OIL TANK

# High-Efficiency Heat Exchangers

PULSE FURNACE HEAT EXCHANGER COMPONENTS

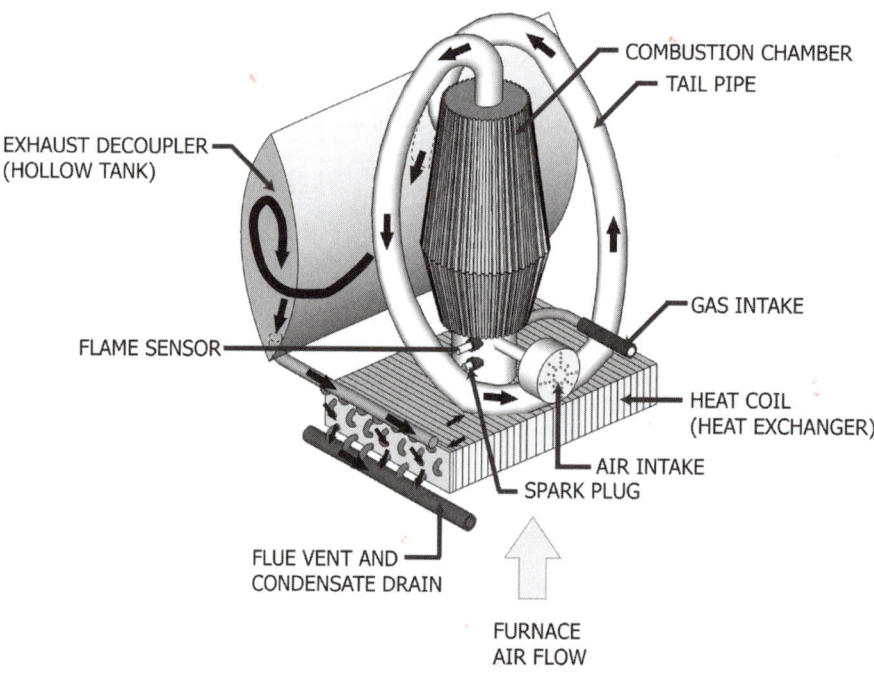

High-efficiency furnaces use the principle that as hot gases cool, they release a lot of heat energy as they change their state from a gas to a liquid. Burning natural gas creates water vapor and carbon dioxide. As we cool the exhaust byproducts, heat is released. If we can cool the vapor into a liquid, a tremendous amount of heat can be extracted.

We can cool that vapor inside a furnace using the heat exchangers. High-efficiency furnaces have at least two heat exchangers. The exchanger inside a high-efficiency furnace is very long — longer than that of a conventional or mid-efficiency furnace. As the hot exhaust gases flow through the long exchanger, the gases cool to the point that they condense. By the time the exhaust combustion gases leave the high-efficiency furnace, the gas temperature could be around 100° F.

Condensation takes place in the second (or third) heat exchanger. That's why they are usually made of stainless steel, because it is more corrosion-resistant. The first heat exchanger is typically made of conventional galvanized steel.

The condensate comes out of the exchanger and drains into tubes or pipes. The condensate may discharge into a drain fitting, a floor drain, a drainpipe, or a condensate pump. It is not good practice to simply drain the condensate through the floor and into the gravel and soil below the concrete floor. The condensate water is slightly acidic. It's not as acidic as vinegar, but some jurisdictions restrict the discharge of the condensate.

When a high-efficiency condensing furnace is operating, a quart of condensate water may drain out every 30 minutes. That's a lot of water.

# Coal, Wood and Multi-Fuel Furnaces

Solid-fuel, forced warm-air furnaces can burn coal or wood. Some multi-fuel furnaces are designed to burn a solid fuel, such as coal, in combination with another fuel, such as oil. In a coal, wood or multi-fuel furnace, the combustion process takes place inside a large sealed firebox. A blower fan circulates air over the heat exchanger and pushes the warm air through ducts or pipes to the rooms and spaces of the building.

## Coal Furnaces

Coal furnaces are either hand-fired or fired with a stoker. Coal has to be brought from the storage to the furnace either by hand or automatically, with a coal-feeding mechanism known as the stoker. Early coal furnaces were gravity systems. Systems built later incorporated blower fans.

The front of a coal furnace should not be blocked. Access to the fire and ash pit doors is required in order to run the furnace. The components of a coal furnace include the:

- cabinet or jacket;
- firebox;
- grate;
- heat exchanger;
- blower fan and motor;
- access door for stoking and cleaning;
- small blower fan to fan the fire;
- coal stoker; and
- automatic controls.

### Wood Furnace

A wood furnace is very similar to a coal furnace except that it burns wood instead of coal. The components and accessories for the two types of furnaces are almost identical.

### Multi-Fuel Furnaces

A furnace that's designed to burn more than one fuel is referred to as a multi-fuel furnace or combination furnace. A combination furnace is able to burn oil or gas in one combustion chamber, and wood or coal in another combustion chamber. It has the ability to switch between the two when desired. The furnace should be serviced and cleaned by a qualified technician on a regular basis to ensure its safe and secure operation. An inspector may check the heat exchanger and smoke pipe. The furnace jacket could be checked for cracks. All access doors should close tightly. The air filter should be clean. Ash and other debris should be removed from the combustion chamber on a daily basis when in regular operation. Heating surfaces of the furnace should be kept clean. Hard clinkers should be removed from the grates.

# Hydronic Heating Systems

A hydronic heating system is a forced hot-water heating system. Water is the heat-conveying medium for hot-water heating systems. Water carries the heat to the rooms and spaces in the house. The hot water circulates in the system by gravity flow, or the water is forced into circulation by a pump. In a typical hot-water heating system, the water is heated in a boiler or water heater unit and circulates through distribution pipes to baseboard convectors or radiators. The boiler or water heater can use various fuels for heating the water, including No. 2 fuel oil, natural gas, propane, coal, electricity, or a solid fuel.

The radiators or baseboards are usually located within rooms and hallways at the outside edge of the structure, along the exterior walls. There may be radiant panels in the floor or ceiling. There may be one or more thermostats installed throughout the house. When the thermostat calls for heat, the boiler or water heater heats the water and sends the hot water into the radiators or baseboards. The heat is released and distributed to the interior using natural convection.

## Identifying and Describing Hot-Water Heating Systems

There are three ways to describe hot-water heating systems using the following broad categories:

- supply water temperature;
- the type of water circulation; and
- the arrangement of the distribution pipes.

## Supply Water Temperature

A hot-water system that supplies hot water at temperatures higher than 250° F is referred to as a high-temperature system. This type of system is usually installed in commercial and industrial buildings. A low-temperature system is one that supplies hot water at temperatures below 250° F, and it's generally installed in residential and small buildings.

## Type of Water Circulation

Every hot-water heating system circulates water either by a pump, as with a forced hot-water heating system, or by gravity, as with a gravity hot-water heating system. Gravity hot-water heating systems rely on gravity and the different weights of water, which are determined by the differences in temperature of the water, similar to the principles related to air temperature. As such, hot water is lighter than cold water.

## Arrangement of the Distribution Pipes

There are four types of distribution-pipe arrangements for a hot-water heating system. They include the:

- one-pipe system;
- series-loop system;
- two-pipe direct-return system; and
- two-pipe reverse-return system.

## ONE-PIPE SYSTEM

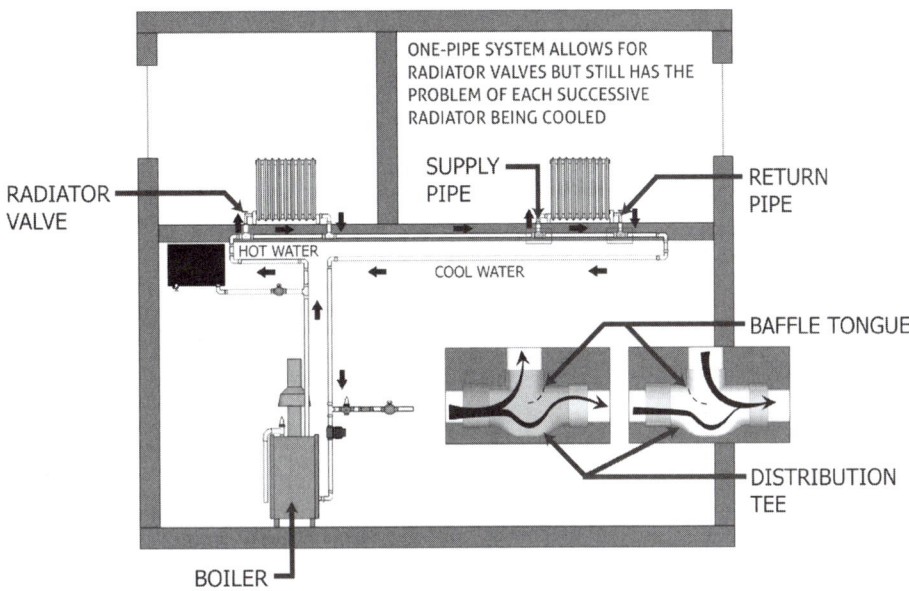

RADIATOR VALVE

ONE-PIPE SYSTEM ALLOWS FOR RADIATOR VALVES BUT STILL HAS THE PROBLEM OF EACH SUCCESSIVE RADIATOR BEING COOLED

SUPPLY PIPE

RETURN PIPE

HOT WATER

COOL WATER

BAFFLE TONGUE

DISTRIBUTION TEE

BOILER

## One-Pipe System

In a one-pipe system, there is one single pipe that carries the hot water throughout the system. That single pipe carries the hot water to the radiators or baseboard convectors, and it also carries the cool water back to the boiler or water-heating unit. Each heat-emitting unit (radiator or baseboard) is connected to this main single pipe with two smaller branch pipes, which are the feed line and the return line.

One-pipe systems can be forced or gravity types.

The main advantage of a one-pipe system is that each radiator or convector can be controlled individually without interfering with the flow of water to the other heat-emitting units. Zoning can be achieved in a one-pipe system by installing a separate loop, a pump (for forced), and another thermostat.

## Series-Loop System

In a series loop, each heat-emitting unit (radiator or baseboard convector) forms an integral part of the loop or piping circuit. When you shut off one unit, then the entire flow of water is stopped. The water travels from the heating system, flows through each heat-emitting unit, and returns to the heating system — all in one continuous loop of pipe. There are no pipe branches. All of the heat-emitting units are connected one after another in a

## SERIES LOOP

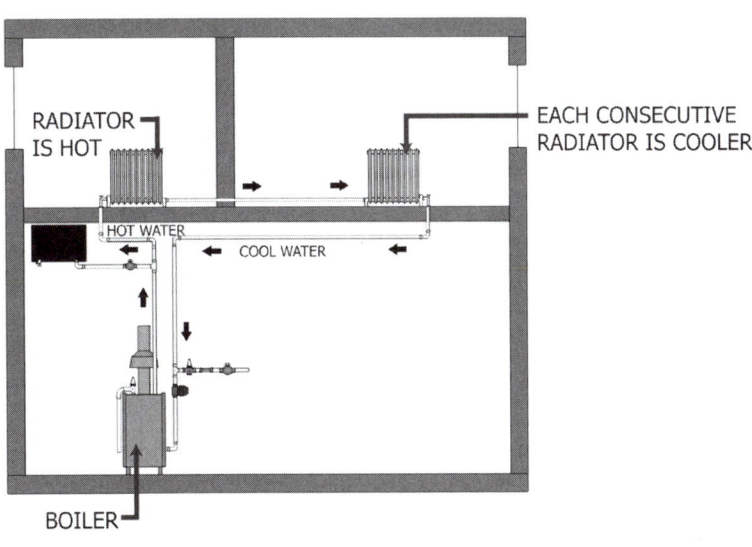

RADIATOR IS HOT

EACH CONSECUTIVE RADIATOR IS COOLER

HOT WATER

COOL WATER

BOILER

series. As a result, the heat-emitting unit that is closest to the heating system is the hottest, and the one farthest away is the coldest. It is not easy to balance this system.

## Two-Pipe Direct-Return System

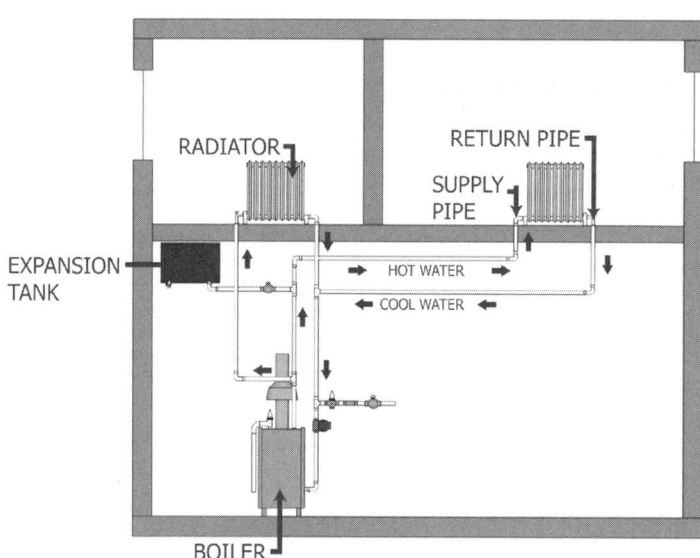

TWO-PIPE SYSTEM (DIRECT RETURN)

In a two-pipe direct-return system, hot water returns to the heating system (boiler or water heater) directly from each heat-emitting unit. Hot water does not pass through any other heat-emitting unit on its way back to the heating unit. The hot water supply pipes and the cool water return pipes are separate pipes. Each heat-emitting unit is connected to the supply and return lines separately.

## Two-Pipe Reverse-Return System

In a two-pipe reverse-return system, a balance is achieved because there are separate circuits for each radiator or baseboard of equal length from the heating unit. Regardless of the location of the heat-emitting unit, the length of pipe in that circuit will be equivalent to any other circuit. In this system, there exists a central main pipe that collects all of the cool return water that comes out of each radiator or baseboard unit before entering the boiler or water heater. The closest radiator in the system has the shortest supply-pipe length and the longest return pipe. The farthest radiator has the longest supply-pipe length and the shortest return-pipe length.

## Combination of Systems

You may see a combination of pipe arrangements in a one-pipe hot-water heating system. You may see a series loop tapped off a two-pipe system.

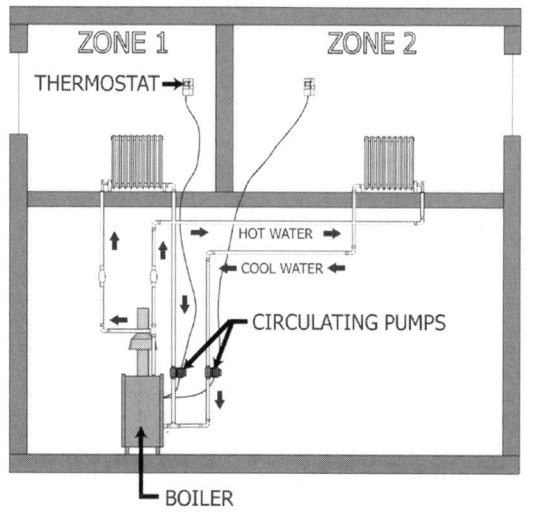

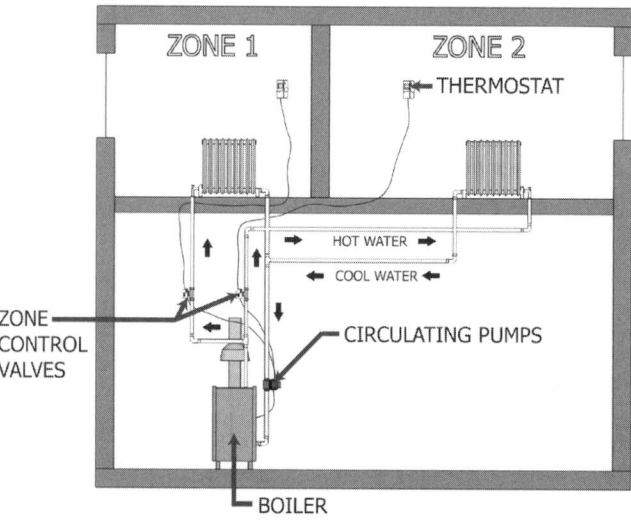

## Zoning

Zoning is achieved by installing valves and thermostats in the hot-water supply pipes. A valve may be wired up to a thermostat that activates that valve and controls that zone. Balancing a system can be achieved by zoning or breaking up a large system into smaller ones that are independently controlled by thermostats.

## Radiant Panels

There may be radiant panel units installed on a hot-water heating system. A radiant panel is considered neither a radiator nor a baseboard convector. The pipes are concealed in the floor, ceiling or wall. The floor, ceiling or wall acts as the heat-emitting unit. An infrared camera comes in handy for inspecting these embedded systems.

## Gravity Hot-Water Heating Systems

You may find a gravity hot-water heating system installed in an older home. You can identify a gravity system by its large-diameter pipes made of wrought iron or black iron. The very large pipes would be the supply lines used to deliver the hot water to the rooms and spaces of the building. The boiler of a gravity hot-water heating system would likely be made of cast iron. You may find that the old boiler was converted from burning coal or wood to oil or gas.

The main method by which the water moves in a gravity hot-water heating system is via the differences in weight of the water at different temperatures. Hot water floats and cold water falls. The difference in weight (the specific gravity) of water at different temperatures moves the water or circulates it throughout the system without the use of a pump. Hot water is light, and cold water is heavy. Gravity systems are sometimes referred to as thermal or natural hot-water heating systems.

The heat supplied to the rooms of a building with a gravity hot-water heating system feels continuous and uniform. The water temperature can be controlled for each heat-emitting unit. The air temperature can be controlled for each room.

The movement of water based upon the principle of gravity and different temperatures is easy to understand. One cubic foot of water at 68° F weighs 62.31 pounds. At 212° F, the water weighs 59.82 pounds. The difference in weight is caused by the expansion of the hot water. Hot water expands. This 2.49-pound difference makes the water circulate through the system because hot water is light and rises, and cold water is heavy and falls. In a gravity hot-water heating system, the cool water falls and pushes the warmer, lighter water upward.

Because water expands when heated, a provision for expansion is needed in hot-water heating systems.

## Forced Hot-Water Heating Systems

The most commonly used methods for forcing hot water to circulate in a system are by pumps, or by a combination of pumps and local boosters. There are other ways of forcing water to circulate in a hot-water heating system, but they are not as common.

They include:

- the use of nipples on each radiator section;
- high pressure to increase temperature differences;
- super-heating a part of the water circulation, and creating and condensing steam; and

• introducing steam into a main riser pipe at the top of a circulating system.

It is common to find one or more pumps as the main method of circulating or forcing hot water in a system.

## Hot-Water Boilers

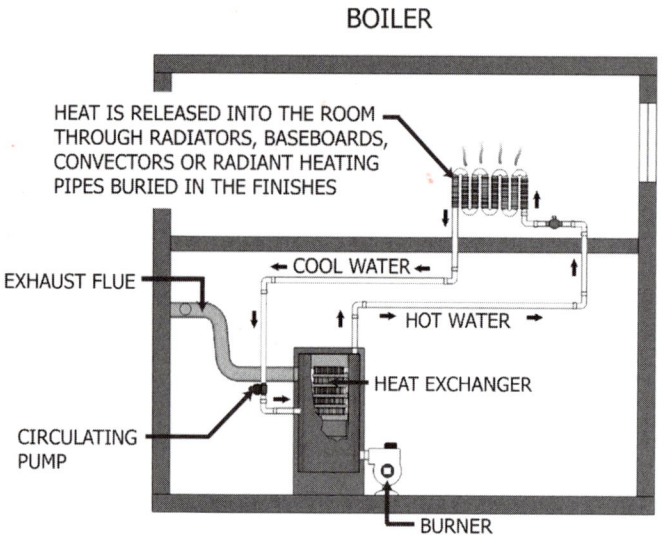

BOILER

HEAT IS RELEASED INTO THE ROOM THROUGH RADIATORS, BASEBOARDS, CONVECTORS OR RADIANT HEATING PIPES BURIED IN THE FINISHES

EXHAUST FLUE
← COOL WATER ←
→ HOT WATER →
HEAT EXCHANGER
CIRCULATING PUMP
BURNER

The boilers of a hot-water heating system that you may inspect may be made of cast iron or steel. Cast iron is more common because cast-iron boilers generally have better resistance to the corrosive effects of water than do steel boilers. Boilers may be fired up with various fuels, including oil, solid fuels, gas (natural or propane), and electricity. On older systems, you may find that the coal boiler was converted to gas or oil. All boilers should be certified and have some label to that effect. There are several organizations that certify boilers.

## Hydronic Furnaces

A hydronic furnace is one that has water heated up initially by a boiler or water heater, and then it's circulated through a heat exchanger inside the furnace's air handler. The heat exchanger is a coil of pipes that transfers liquid-to-air heat. Heat is transferred from the water in the coils to the air that passes through the furnace's air handler. A blower fan circulates the air through the coil. The heated air comes out of the furnace and is distributed to the structure through ducts or pipes. This installation is sometimes referred to as a hydro-air heating system.

## Combination Water Heaters

A combination water heater can produce both hot water for heating the building and hot water for heating the domestic hot-water supply at the same time. There is either a tank or a coil immersed inside the hot water of the boiler. The hot water of the boiler indirectly heats the water of the inner tank or coil.

The boiler water transfers its heat by conduction to the domestic water supply in the inner tank or coil. The two supplies of water (the water in

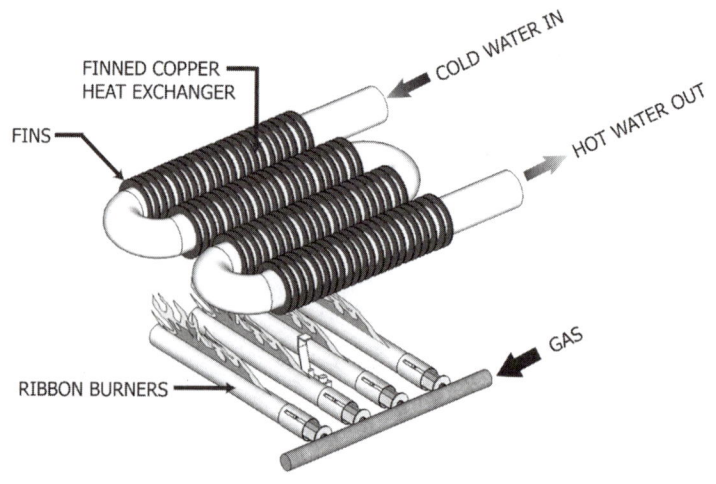

COPPER TUBE HEAT EXCHANGERS

FINNED COPPER HEAT EXCHANGER
FINS
COLD WATER IN
HOT WATER OUT
GAS
RIBBON BURNERS

the boiler and the water in the inner tank or coil) are completely separate from each other. There's no mixing or contamination. A combination water heater may incorporate the use of a circulating pump, expansion tank, pressure-reducing fill valve, and a zone valve. A combination water heater may also use steam to heat the domestic hot-water supply.

## Control Components

There are two types of control components for a hot-water heating system. One type is for system-actuating, and the other type is for safety. System-actuating controls include the thermostat, burner controls, and pump controls.

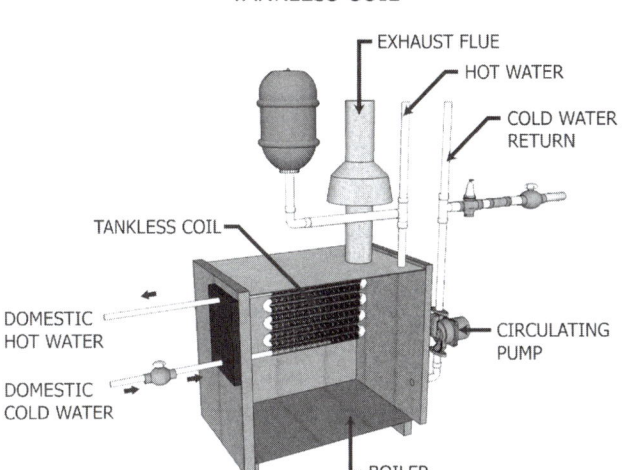

TANKLESS COIL

EXHAUST FLUE
HOT WATER
COLD WATER RETURN
TANKLESS COIL
DOMESTIC HOT WATER
DOMESTIC COLD WATER
CIRCULATING PUMP
BOILER

HIGH TEMPERATURE LIMIT SWITCH

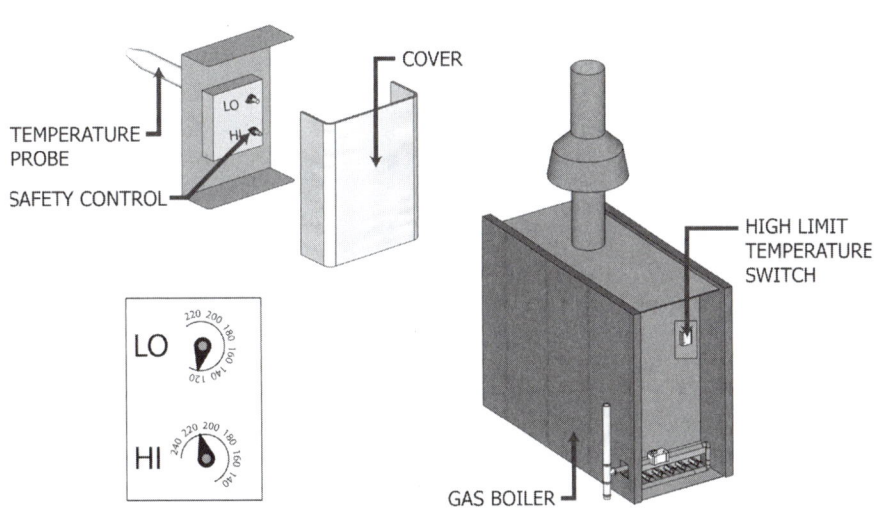

COVER
TEMPERATURE PROBE
SAFETY CONTROL
LO
HI
HIGH LIMIT TEMPERATURE SWITCH
GAS BOILER

Safety controls include high-limit controls, pressure-relief valves, and pressure-reducing valves. Safety controls prevent damage to the system and may prevent the risk of injuring people by shutting down the system when the pressure and/or temperature levels become excessive. A high-limit control is a device that shuts down the system if the pressure or temperature of the hot water exceeds a certain limit.

Another safety control is a pressure-relief valve. A pressure-relief valve opens up and releases pressure when the water pressure inside the boiler exceeds a certain limit. Pressure-relief valves are required to be installed on all boilers and water-heating systems.

TEMPERATURE AND PRESSURE GAUGE

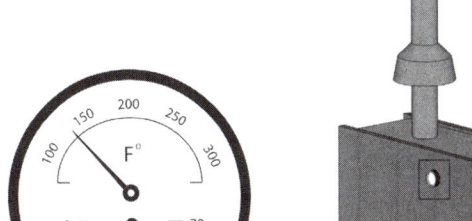

## Pipes

The pipes of a hydronic system may be made of cast iron, wrought iron, copper, steel, plastic or rubber. The diameter-size of the pipe is dependent upon various factors, including the water's flow rate, and the friction inside the pipe material.

## Expansion Tanks

Expansion tanks are necessary on hot-water heating systems because hot water expands. The tank provides a way to absorb the expansion of the water being heated, and it assists in the contraction of the water as it cools. When water in the system heats up, it expands into the tank. Excess water expands into the expansion tank.

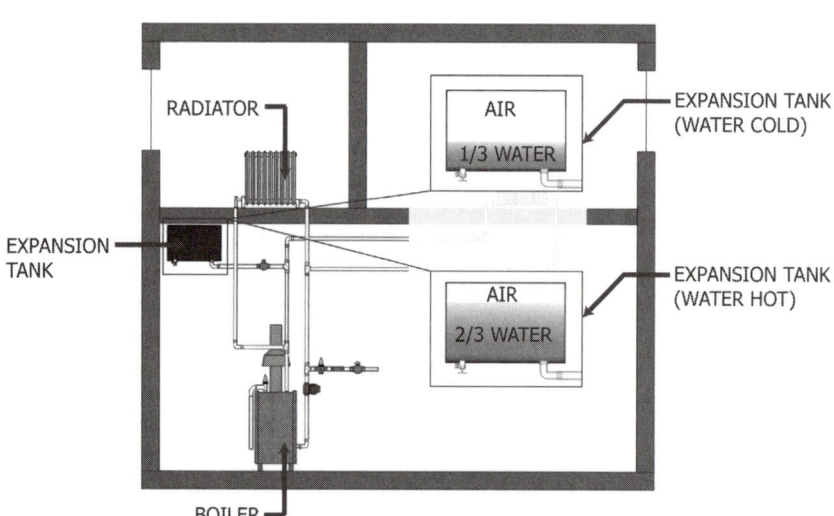

EXPANSION TANK WATER LEVELS

Why is the expansion tank always found above the heating system? An added benefit or function of an expansion tank is that the boiling point of the water can be raised by elevating the tank. When you elevate or raise an expansion tank, you increase the head, which is a term used to describe the difference in elevation between two points in a body of fluid. When you increase the head, you increase the pressure. This results in the ability to heat water at a significantly higher temperature without generating steam. The more heat that is supplied to the heat-emitting units, the better. That is why you will always see an expansion tank over the boiler.

According to Boyles' Law, at a constant temperature, the pressure of a gas varies inversely to its volume. When the volume is reduced, the pressure increases inversely proportionately. If the volume of air inside an expansion tank decreases by half, then the pressure increases by a factor of 2. (This refers to absolute pressure, not gauge pressure.)

On older gravity systems, you may find an open expansion tank. Open tanks are used on low-pressure systems, such as gravity systems. A closed tank is installed on high-

CLOSED HYDRONIC SYSTEM

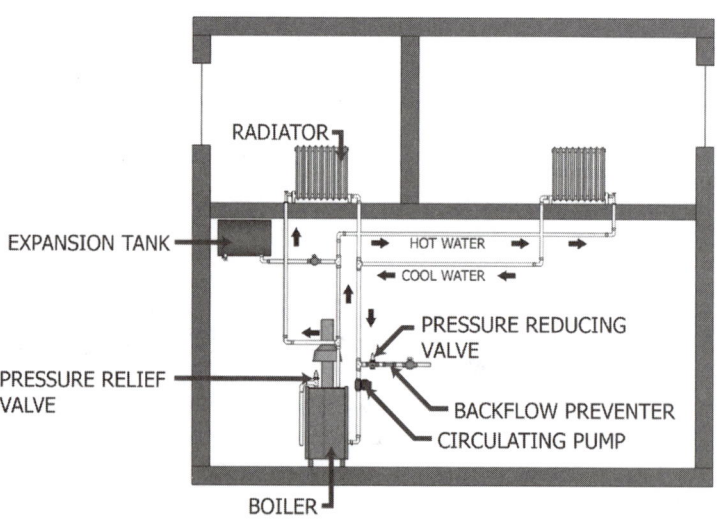

pressure hydronic heating systems. As the temperature of the water increases, the water in the system expands. As the water expands, water enters the tank. In a closed system, the expansion tank has air that is compressed and, as a result, the pressure in the system is increased. On a closed system, it is important to look for the required pressure-relief valve.

## Circulating Pumps

Circulating pumps are used to circulate hot water in a hydronic forced hot-water heating system. They push the water through the piping system. The pump should be placed in the correct position on the heating system in order to be effective. Manufacturers usually describe the proper location of the pump in the unit's installation manual.

## Heat-Emitting Units

Heat-emitting units are the radiators, baseboard convectors, and other heat-emitting components from which the heat is transferred into the room and spaces of the building. Cast-iron radiators are common in older systems. They may be located on the floor or even hung on the wall. The radiators may be recessed inside a wall, or partially covered or enclosed by a cabinet structure. If the radiator is covered, there should be openings provided at the top and bottom of the covering or cabinet to allow air to circulate.

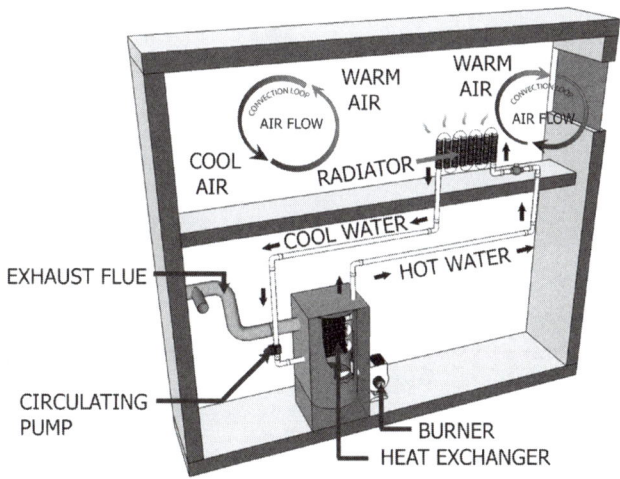

CONVECTION HEAT THROUGH RADIATOR

Convectors are tubes with fins on them. The finned tubes are enclosed in a cabinet or baseboard unit with openings at the top and the bottom.

As the hot water moves through the tubes, the fins get hot and radiate heat. Room air enters the cabinet or baseboard from the bottom, and exits from the top through openings.

Radiant floor units may be made of flexible tubing installed directly below the floor. The heat is transferred from the tubing into the floor surface. Flexible tubes and radiant panels are also used as heat-emitting units in ceilings and walls.

## Electric Hydronic Heating Systems

Hydronic heating systems may use electricity to heat the water. Electric hydronic heating systems are usually compact electric boilers or water heaters, available in various small sizes.

## Advantages of Hydronic Heating Systems

There are many advantages of hydronic heating systems. The heat is uniformly delivered. Less energy is used to circulate water through pipes than is needed to circulate air through a duct system. It is easy to zone a hydronic heating system. The indoor air quality issues are reduced because there is no air agitation as there is with a forced warm-air system.

## Boiler Control Devices

Steam and hot-water (hydronic) heating boilers look similar, but there are several important differences.

- Steam boilers operate at about three-quarters full of water.
- Hot-water boilers operate full of water.
- Steam boilers in homes operate at around 2 psi (or slightly more).
- Hot-water boilers operate at six times that (12 psi).
- A steam boiler has a low-water cutoff device.
- Hot-water boilers in homes likely don't have a low-water cutoff device.
- Steam boilers need a water feed to replace water lost through evaporation and steam.
- Hot-water boilers have little or no need for makeup water.

Most of the controls on low-pressure steam and hot-water boilers (fired by the same fuel) are similar, but there are exceptions.

Many different types of controls are required on hot-water heating systems. They are either system-actuating controls (thermostats, burner controls, pump controls) or safety controls (high-limit switches, pressure-relief valves, pressure-reducing valves).

## Safety Controls

Safety controls shut down the system to prevent damage, particularly when the temperature and pressure limits are exceeded. A high-limit control on a hot-water boiler will help shut down the system if the pressure or temperature of the hot water exceeds pre-set limits.

## Pressure-Relief Valves

Pressure-relief valves are important safety controls for hot-water heating systems. When the pressure inside a boiler reaches a certain point, the pressure-relief valve will open up. It closes when the boiler pressure returns to a lower, safe level. Pressure-relief valves are required to be installed on hot-water heating systems. Check with your local building code authority.

## Pressure-Relief Valve on Steam Systems

A pressure-relief valve (or valves) must be installed on a steam boiler. It's sometimes referred to by the inspector as a safety valve or safety relief valve. The pressure-relief valve will open up and release excess steam at or below the maximum allowable working pressure of the boiler. On low-pressure boilers that you'll find in homes, the pressure-relief valve will likely be set to open and release steam when a maximum pressure of 15 psi is reached in the boiler. The valve should automatically close when the pressure falls back down to normal levels again.

## Steam-Heating Devices

Boilers used for steam-heating systems have devices designed for (a) measuring or indicating, and (b) control. Steam boilers should have installed on them the following:

- water level gauge;
- low-water cutoff;

- pressure gauge;
- safety relief valve; and
- high-pressure limit switch.

A water level gauge measures the boiler's water level. A low-water cutoff device automatically shuts off the burner if the water level of the boiler is too low. The pressure gauge measures the operating pressure inside the boiler. The safety relief valve discharges excess steam when the pressure inside the boiler exceeds a maximum safe working pressure on the valve. The burner shuts off by the high-pressure limit switch when the boiler pressure exceeds a pre-set level.

## Two Types of Steam-Heating Systems

There are basically two types of steam-heating systems: low-pressure and high-pressure. The type depends upon the operating pressure of the steam in the system. Low-pressure steam systems typically are set to operate at a pressure of 0 to 15 psig. High-pressure steam systems operate in excess of 15 psig. You'll usually find low-pressure steam systems installed in homes.

## Hot-Water Boilers

Hot-water boilers have a variety of valves, controls and devices. Some are similar to those found on a steam boiler, but there are significant differences. Hot-water boilers operate under high pressures and temperatures.

Inspectors can look for the following devices installed on hot-water boilers:

- pressure-relief valve, which relieves a boiler of excessive pressure;
- low-water cutoff, which switches off the burner if the boiler's water level drops too low;
- high-pressure limit switch, which turns off the burner when the boiler pressure exceeds its pre-set maximum safe operating level;
- aquastat, which automatically controls the temperature limits and operates the circulator pump(s);
- water pressure-reducing valve, which keeps the boiler filled with water;
- air vent, which releases air from the system;
- expansion tank, which takes the expanded volume of heated water in the system;
- air separator, which traps air bubbles from the water before it's circulated in the system; and
- circulator pump, which moves water through the system.

## Pressure-Relief Valve on Boilers

Inspectors should look for a pressure-relief valve that is rated higher than the maximum working pressure of the boiler. The boiler could explode if it exceeds its maximum working pressure with this incorrect valve installed on it. The valve relieves pressure created by (a) water thermal conditions, and (b) steam pressure conditions. Relief valves help prevent personal injury and property damage. These valves open at a pre-set pressure. As the pressure drops, the valve closes. When the water pressure reaches a certain point, the valve functions as a water-relief valve and discharges water that has expanded in the system. This valve may also relieve and discharge steam when it's present inside the hot-water boiler, which is an indication of a malfunctioning firing control.

## High-Pressure Limit Switch

This device is used for safety and will shut down the burner when the boiler's pressure exceeds a pre-set level (commonly 5 to 8 psi). The high-pressure limit switch is connected to the boiler by a pigtail pipe.

## Aquastat

The aquastat, or high-limit control, is a safety control that helps prevent damage to the boiler by shutting it down. It works with the circulator pump(s). It can be strapped to the hot-water supply riser or mounted on the boiler so that its heat-sensitive element is immersed inside the boiler. If the pressure or temperature of the hot water exceeds the certain limit of the system, the system shuts down.

## Pressure-Reducing Valves

Most hot-water boilers have water pressure-reducing valves, which feed water into the boiler automatically when the pressure in the system drops. It keeps the system automatically filled with water. It's installed on the cold-water supply line. Older systems may have a manually operated feed valve. Water pressure-reducing valves are usually set to feed water to the boiler at about 15 pounds of pressure, which is usually sufficient for a house no more than three stories high. Combination valves (or dual-control valves) are installed on hot-water boilers, and they combine a pressure-reducing/pressure-regulating valve and a positive relief valve in one device. This combination valve can regulate pressure, control safety, reduce boiler pressure, and auto-fill the boiler. If the expansion is waterlogged or has a problem with expanding water, the relief valve will open at 23 psi to drop the pressure back down, and will close when the pressure drops below 14 psi.

## Low-Water Cutoff on Boilers

A low-water cutoff must be installed on boilers. This device shuts off the burner when the water level in the boiler drops to a level too low for safe operation. Two types of low-water cutoff devices are float and probe. All residential steam boilers must have a low-water cutoff device installed.

## Blowdown Valve on Boilers

A blowdown valve is used to remove sediment and contaminants in the water of the boiler, near the low point of the bottom of the boiler. Over time, these sediments and contaminants in the water of the boiler will settle there. The blowdown valve should be opened to drain off the sediments as part of a regular maintenance routine.

# Quiz #7

1. T/F: Air is the heat-conveying medium for hydronic heating systems.

☐ True
☑ False

2. One cubic foot of water at 68° F weighs about ____ pounds.

☑ 62
☐ 47
☐ 26

3. T/F: Radiators and baseboard convectors are considered heat-emitting components.

☑ True
☐ False

**Answer Key is on page 118.**

# Steam-Heating Systems

Steam can be used as a heat-conveying medium. Steam-heating systems are not commonly found in modern homes. You may find that the steam systems in small commercial buildings have been replaced by other types of heating systems that operate more efficiently and less expensively.

In a steam-heating system, the boiler turns water into steam. The steam rises through pipes to the heat-emitting units. Inside the units, the steam cools and condenses into water. The condensate water returns to the boiler, and the cycle begins again.

## Identifying and Describing Steam-Heating Systems

There are a few ways to identify and describe a steam-heating system. The description of a steam-heating system may include the following:

- the pressure and vacuum conditions (low or high);
- how the condensate water returns to the boiler (gravity or mechanical);
- the piping (one-pipe or two-pipe);
- the type of piping circuit (divided, one-pipe, or loop);
- the direction of steam in the risers (upfeed or downfeed); and
- the location of the condensate returns (dry return or wet return).

## Gravity Steam-Heating Systems

The distinguishing characteristic of a gravity steam-heating system is that the condensate returns to the boiler from the heat-emitting units by gravity rather than by some mechanical means.

## One-Pipe Gravity Steam

In a one-pipe steam-heating system, the steam is carried around the lowest level of the building — typically, a basement. From that main circuit, branches to each individual heat-emitting unit are taken off. In a one-pipe system, the condensate returns to the boiler through the main steam supply pipe. Both steam and condensate are in that pipe. The main is sloped back toward the boiler. The pipe is sloped from the immediate high point located near and above the boiler to the bottom of the boiler, usually entering the side of the boiler.

## Two-Pipe Gravity Steam

In a two-pipe system, the steam and the condensate are separated into two different pipes. Steam comes from the boiler, rises up through the supply pipes, heat is emitted, steam is condensed in the heat-emitting units, and the condensate water returns back through return pipes to the boiler.

## Steam Boilers

A steam boiler heats water until it boils and changes into steam. A steam boiler can run on various types of fuel. Steam comes from the boiler, rises up through pipes, and enters the heat-emitting units. The design and construction of a steam boiler is very similar to a boiler for a hot-water heating system.

## Control Components

The control components for a steam boiler are similar to those used in a hot-water heating system.

The controls for a steam boiler include the:

- safety valve;
- steam pressure gauge;
- low-water cutoff;
- water-fill feeder;
- pressure high-limit control;
- water gauge glass; and
- primary control.

## Hartford Return

A steam-heating system should have a Hartford return connection, often referred to as a Hartford loop. The Hartford return is installed on the condensate return line. It prevents total loss of water from the boiler if there is a water leak in the return line.

An equalizer connects the lower outlet to the steam outlet. The Hartford return is connected to the equalizer about 2 inches below the normal water level of the steam boiler.

## Steam Traps

A steam trap is a device installed on a steam line that controls the flow of steam, air and condensate. It automatically opens and discharges air and condensation. It will automatically close to stop steam from escaping.

## Pumps

Pumps are used on steam-heating systems to handle condensate and to discharge excess air.

## Heat-Emitting Units for Steam-Heating Systems

There are two types of heat-emitting units used in steam-heating systems: radiators and convectors. A radiator primarily uses radiation to transmit heat. A convector primarily uses convection to transmit heat. A convector is usually made of a tube with fins attached.

## Unit Heaters

A unit heater (sometimes called a space heater) is essentially a convector with a fan. The fan forces air over the heating element or surface. The warm air is discharged into the room or space.

## Water Hammer

"Water hammer" is a problem in a steam-heating system that occurs when condensed water is trapped in a section of a horizontal steam pipe. The steam pipes should be sloped properly. Steam bubbles may get trapped in the return lines and then the bubbles will start imploding in the water-filled wet-return lines, causing the noise known as water hammer. Properly sized gravity return lines are needed to allow sufficient room for the steam to flow in the top of the pipe without mixing with the condensate flowing on the bottom of the pipe.

# Electric Heating Systems

There are various types of electric heating systems. They all use electricity to transfer heat by the following three ways:

- radiation;
- convection; and
- forced air.

## Electric Hot-Water Systems

An electric boiler may be used as a home's main heat source. Electric boilers are compact and insulated, with heating elements immersed in the water of the boiler. Inside the compact electric boiler unit are all of the components, including the expansion tank, pump, valves and controls.

## Electric Forced Warm-Air Heating Systems

At an electric forced warm-air heating system, heated air is forced through to the rooms and spaces of the building by the use of a blower fan and ducts or pipes. They have zero clearances. They can be installed horizontally or vertically. Inside the electric furnace is at least one coiled resistance-wire heating element. If there is more than one coil, the coils are activated sequentially, one by one, to prevent an electrical current overload. There is a high-temperature control installed in the unit. The furnace is controlled by a thermostat. A blower fan is installed to force air through the heating elements.

## Electrical Radiant Heating Systems

A common type of electrical radiant heating system is one that has a cable embedded in the floor, wall or ceiling. The heat that is created by the cable is transferred to the occupants and surfaces in the room by low-intensity radiation.

There are three types of radiant panel systems:

- radiant floor panel systems;
- radiant wall panel systems; and
- radiant ceiling panel systems.

## Electric Baseboard Heating Systems

Electric baseboard heating units are usually installed at floor level at the perimeter of each room or space of the building, particularly below windows.

An electric baseboard is made of a heating element protected by a thin metal housing. Heat is transferred into the room primarily by means of convection, although some radiation is involved. A thermostat may be mounted on a wall or built into the unit. Air moves across the electric baseboard and heat is transferred from the heating element to the air. Electric baseboard heating systems are the most common type of electric heating.

## Heat Pumps

A heat pump is an electrically powered system that has a reversible-cycle refrigeration system that is capable of both heating and cooling the interior air of a building. The heat source is either air (as in air-to-air heat pump systems) or water (as in water-to-air heat pump systems). The most common type for residential installations is the air-to-air heat pump system.

# Steam and Hot-Water Space-Heating Systems

Boilers supply hot water or steam to heat buildings. The boilers that we see in residences are low-pressure steam and hot-water (hydronic) space-heating boilers. These boilers are fired up with fossil fuels. They have an insulated steel jacket on the outside, a lower chamber where combustion takes place, and an upper chamber where the heat exchanger is located. That is where the water is heated or turned into steam. The steam or hot water is then circulated throughout the building through distribution boiler pipes.

Steam boilers are not completely full of water. They are only about 75% full. A hot-water boiler is completely filled with water.

Steam boilers run at about 2 psi. Hot-water boilers operate at about 12 to 15 psi.

All steam boilers are required to have a low-water cutoff device. Hot-water boilers are usually not required to have one.

Steam boilers require fresh water to be added to the system at regular intervals because they lose water due to evaporation and steam. Hot-water boilers typically do not require the regular addition of fresh water to the system.

## HEAT EXCHANGER

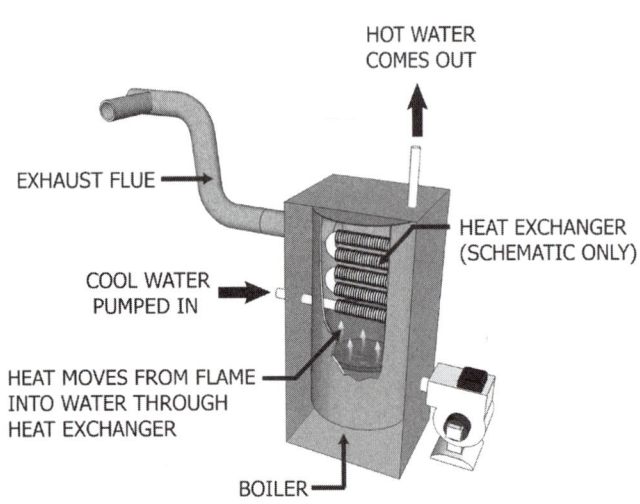

HOT WATER COMES OUT

EXHAUST FLUE

HEAT EXCHANGER (SCHEMATIC ONLY)

COOL WATER PUMPED IN

HEAT MOVES FROM FLAME INTO WATER THROUGH HEAT EXCHANGER

BOILER

The construction and design of steam and hot-water boilers are similar. The combustion chamber differs for each type of boiler according to the different types of fuel that the boiler is designed to burn. Oil boilers have oil burners that are mounted on the outside of the combustion chamber. Gas boilers have gas burner assemblies that are located inside the combustion chamber.

The upper chamber of a boiler contains cast-iron sections or steel tubes. Water is inside the cast-iron section or steel tubes. This water gets heated by the combustion taking place below in the lower chamber (the combustion chamber). The heat from the combustion taking place in the lower chamber is transferred to the cast-iron sections or steel tubes that contain water and to the water inside. In a hot-water boiler, the water completely fills the cast-iron sections or steel tubes. In a steam boiler, only the lower two-thirds are filled with water.

In a steam boiler, water is heated rapidly to the point when steam is created. That hot steam rises up through the distribution pipes and supplies heat to the building.

## Boiler Efficiency

Boiler efficiency is based on several factors, including the type of fuel used, the method of firing, and the control settings. The efficiency rating of a boiler is measured by its annual fuel utilization efficiency (AFUE). The minimum established by the U.S. government for boilers is 78%. Mid-efficiency boilers have a range of 78 to 82%. High-efficiency (condensing) boilers range from 88 to 97%. Conventional (non-condensing) steam and hot-water space-heating boilers have AFUE ranges of around 60 to 65%.

## Describing Boilers

Low-pressure boilers and hot-water space heaters can be identified and described in variety of ways. Such boilers can be categorized by:

- cast iron or steel;
- type of exchanger;
- type of fuel used; and
- one or two pipes.

Most boilers are made of cast iron or steel. A few are made of aluminum. Cast-iron boilers typically last longer because cast iron resists corrosion better than steel. The heat exchanger of many boilers is made up of sections of cast-iron pieces that are joined together either in layers horizontally ("sandwiched" or "pancaked" together) or vertically, like a tight stack of dominos. The water moves from section to section in a zigzag pattern and gets heated.

In boilers with a tubular heat exchanger, the water either circulates within the tubes and gets heated by the combustion gases, or the water circulates around the tubes that contain the hot combustion gases.

A hot-water copper-fin tube operates slightly differently than cast-iron and steel boilers. Water flows across the fins and gets heated very quickly.

Boilers can be fired by various fuels or means, including electricity. The most common boilers tend to be gas-fired or oil-fired.

## Steam Boiler Valves and Controls

Boilers used for steam heat have a variety of valves and controls. They can be divided into two broad categories: safety and measurement; and controlling.

Steam boilers may have the following components installed on them:

- a water-level gauge, which measures the water level in the boiler;
- a low-water cutoff, which is a device that turns the boiler off if the water level gets too low;
- a pressure gauge, which measures the operating pressure inside the boiler;
- a pressure-relief valve, which discharges excess steam when the pressure in the boiler exceeds a pre-set limit; and
- a high-pressure limit switch, which shuts off the burner when the boiler reaches a high-pressure limit.

## Pressure/Safety-Relief Valves

On a low-pressure boiler that you may find in a home, the pressure-relief valve should be set to open at a pressure of 15 psi. The pressure-relief valve should not be rated higher than 15 psi. The pressure valve should not have a rating higher than the maximum working pressure of the boiler. You don't want the boiler to rupture under high pressure; you want the valve to activate before that happens.

## PRESSURE-REDUCING VALVE AND PRESSURE-RELIEF VALVE

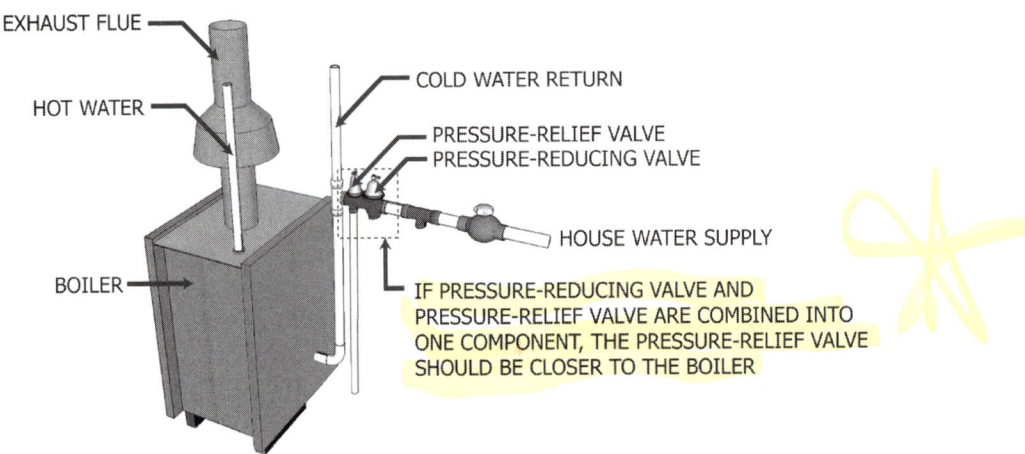

Pressure-relief valves that are installed on a hot-water heating boiler will open under two conditions:

- water thermal conditions; and
- steam-pressure conditions.

## PRESSURE REDUCING VALVE

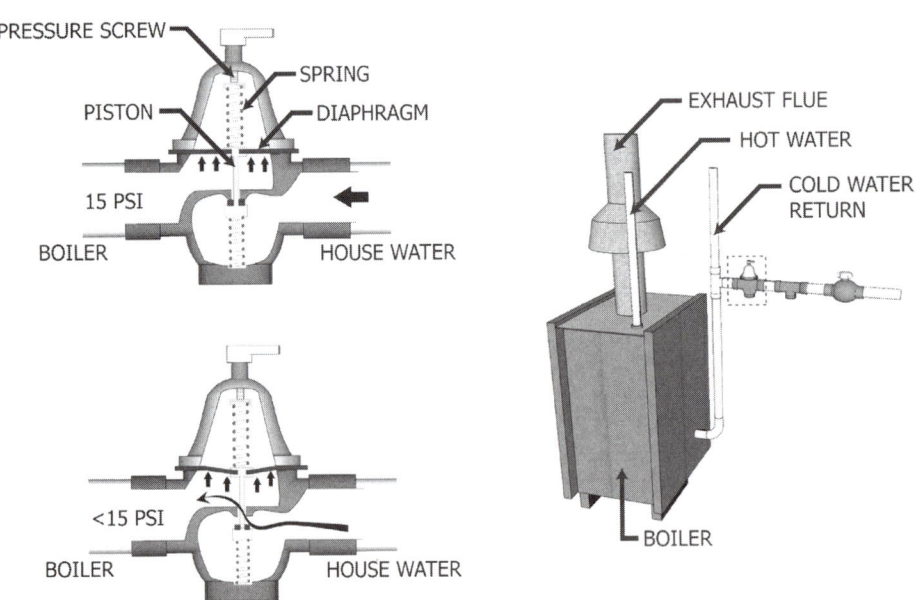

These relief valves are used to protect against damage to property and injury to people. They will start to open up at a pre-set pressure and will open fully at a maximum pressure.

If temperature limits are reached in the boiler, the valve will start to open. If pressure in the boiler reaches a certain limit, the valve opens as a water-relief valve discharges a small amount of water that has expanded inside the boiler.

If both water and steam are present in a hot-water boiler, there is a problem with the boiler. The boiler is reaching steam-forming temperatures, and steam pressure is being created. The relief valve will open under this steam-pressure condition. It acts as a steam-pressure relief valve under this condition in the boiler. These safety-relief valves open under excessive water-pressure conditions and under excessive steam-pressure conditions.

## Pressure-Reducing Valves

Pressure-reducing valves are sometimes referred to as boiler feed valves. Pressure-reducing valves are designed to fill a hot-water boiler automatically if the pressure in the system drops below the setting of the valve. Its primary function is to keep the system automatically filled with water at the desired operating pressure. Older systems have valves that are operated manually. The valve is usually installed on the cold-water supply line.

**PRESSURE RELIEF VALVE**

SPRING

TO DRAIN

PRESSURE LESS
THAN VALVE
RATING

MANUAL RELIEF
LEVER

POPPET
VALVE

TO DRAIN

PRESSURE
GREATER THAN
VALVE RATING

## Combination Valves

Combination valves are used in hot-water boiler systems. They combine a pressure-reducing valve and a relief valve in one device. They provide pressure regulation and the automatic filling of water under certain conditions.

## Blowdown Valve

Sediments will settle at the bottom of the boiler. Sediments can be removed by using a blowdown valve. The valve is installed at the bottom of the boiler. The blowdown valve should be operated periodically to drain the sediments from the boiler.

**BACKFLOW PREVENTER**

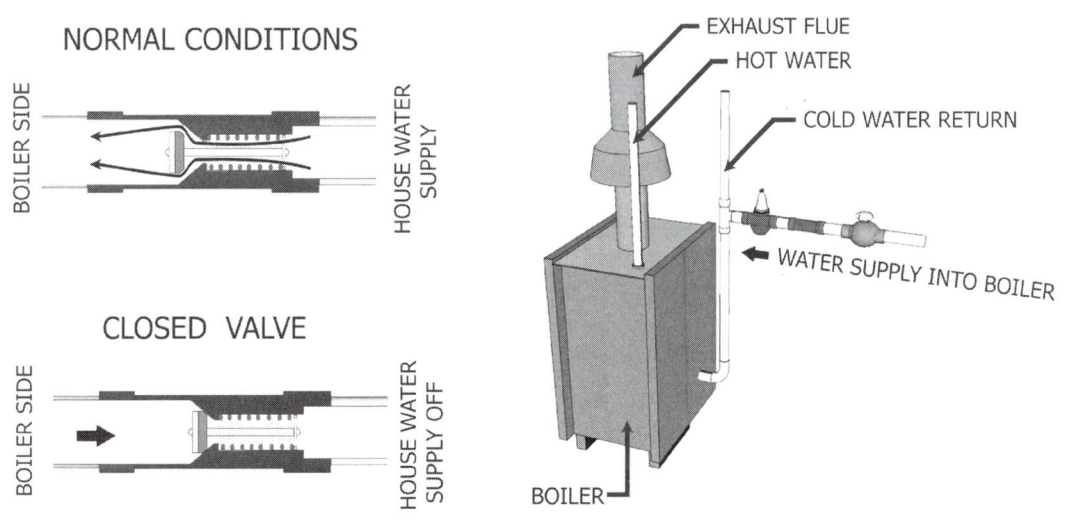

NORMAL CONDITIONS

BOILER SIDE

HOUSE WATER SUPPLY

CLOSED VALVE

BOILER SIDE

HOUSE WATER SUPPLY OFF

EXHAUST FLUE
HOT WATER
COLD WATER RETURN
WATER SUPPLY INTO BOILER
BOILER

## Water Gauges

A water gauge is used to visually check the level of the water in the boiler. The water level should be somewhere between 60 to 75% full. A safe operating level of water varies slightly among different manufacturers of boilers. If the water level appears to be low or empty, then do not operate the boiler. Turn it off, and recommend that it be serviced, including refilling the water using caution. Adding water to a hot boiler could cause damage.

## Backflow Preventer

The unwanted mixing of the water supply to the boiler and the domestic water supply to the house is prevented with a backflow preventer.

## Circulating Pumps

Circulating pumps are used to circulate hot water in a hydronic forced hot-water heating system. They push the water through the piping system. The pump should be placed in the correct position on the heating system in order to be effective. Manufacturers usually describe the proper location of the pump in their installation manual.

## Hartford Return

A steam-heating system should have a Hartford return connection, often referred to as a Hartford loop. The Hartford return is installed on the condensate return line. It prevents total loss of water from the boiler if there is a water leak in the return line. An equalizer connects the lower outlet to the steam outlet. The Hartford return is connected to the equalizer about 2 inches below the normal water level of the steam boiler.

## Air Separator

An air separator traps and removes air bubbles from the water in the boiler system. When a hot-water heating system is filled with cold water, the water contains some air. Air bubbles are created when the water heats up and moves rapidly through the pipes and radiators. The bubbles make noise when they pass through these components. Sometimes a radiator will not heat up because there is a lot of air trapped inside it. An air separator is designed to remove those air bubbles from the system.

Some boilers have air separators designed into them. The air is trapped, separated, and diverted to an automatic air vent at the top of the boiler's separator. Sometimes the air is diverted into the expansion tank above the boiler.

## Expansion Tanks

A hot-water heating system has an expansion tank installed on it. There are two types of tanks: steel tanks and diaphragm tanks.

The primary function of the expansion tank in a hot-water heating system is to provide a space for the expanding water to move into. When the water in the system is heated, its volume may increase by as much as 5%. Tanks limit increases in pressure to the allowable operating/working pressure of the system. They also maintain minimum operating pressures.

The maximum pressure in the boiler system is maintained by the pressure-relief valve. Minimum pressure is maintained by a water-fill valve.

In residential installations, closed steel tanks and diaphragm tanks are used to control the expansion of heated water inside a hot-water heating system.

## Closed Steel Tanks

The closed steel tank has no diaphragm and no moving parts. It is simply filled with water (about two-thirds) and air (about one-third). When the boiler heats up the water, the water expands and enters the tank. As the water enters the tank, the air inside the tank gets compressed. The compression of the air inside the tank results in an increase of system pressure. That pressure can be measured at the pressure gauge of the boiler.

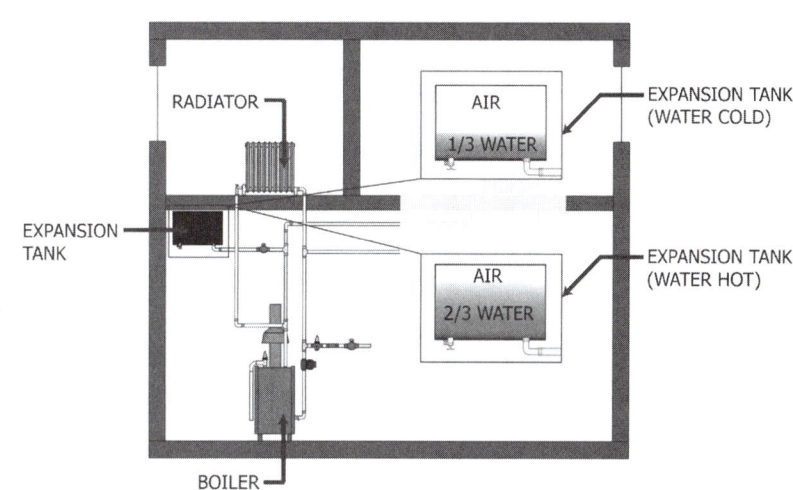

EXPANSION TANK WATER LEVELS

When the water cools down, the water in the system contracts, and the water in the tank releases back into the system. The rise and fall of pressure in the system are related to the expansion and contraction of the air in the expansion tank.

## Diaphragm Expansion Tanks

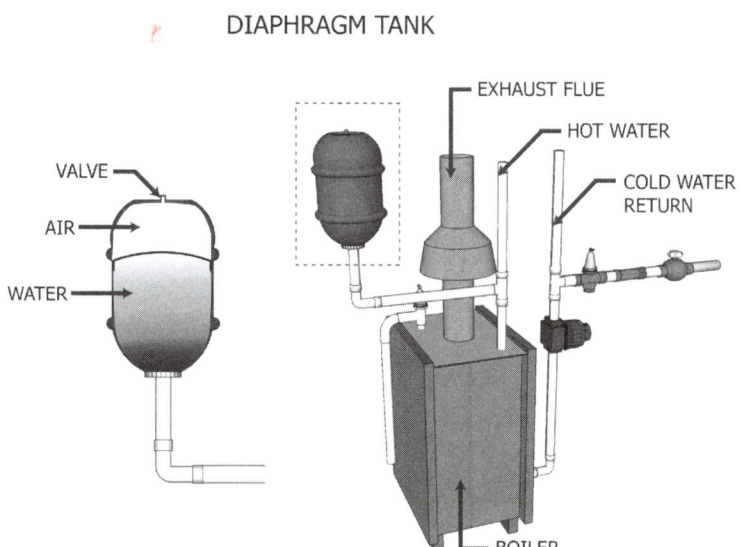

DIAPHRAGM TANK

Inside a diaphragm expansion tank, there is a flexible rubber membrane. The function of this membrane is to prevent air from becoming absorbed into the water, a process that could cause the expansion tank to lose its ability to act as a sort of shock absorber. Over time, if the bladder begins to leak some air, a Schrader valve, identical to the fill valve found on bicycle and car tires, can be used to add more air.

A diaphragm tank is much smaller than a closed steel tank. Most of them come from the manufacturer pre-charged at 12 psi.

A diaphragm tank that is waterlogged will cause the boiler pressure to reach excessive levels. Under this condition, the relief valve will likely begin to drip water. A general rule of thumb for the size of an expansion tank is that there should be 1 gallon for every 3,500 BTU of radiation at heat-emitting units.

## Water-Tempering Valves

Water-tempering valves are used at hot-water heating systems that heat domestic hot water at the boiler. The water-tempering valve mixes hot and cold water to the desired, safe temperature, thus preventing scalding at the fixtures. Without a water-tempering valve, the scalding hot water that is produced at the boiler would be supplied directly from the boiler to the fixtures. These valves are installed at tankless heaters, boiler coils, water heaters, and space-heating systems.

## Balancing Valve

A balancing valve is used to balance a heating system. It can also be used to determine how much water is flowing through the valve.

# Air Conditioning

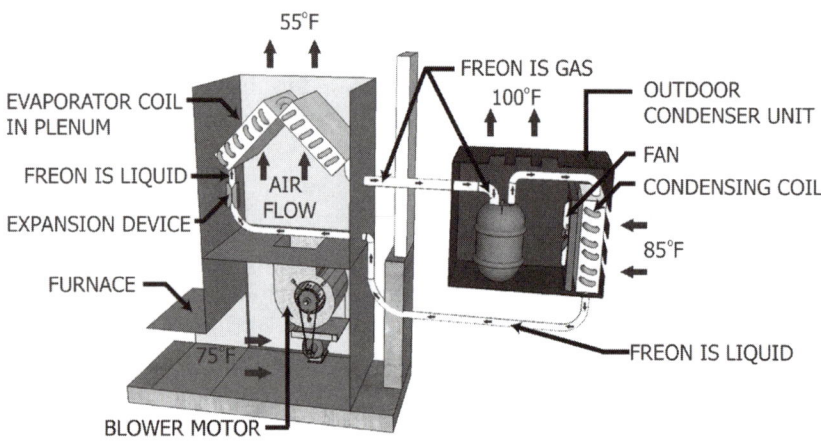

AIR CONDITIONING SYSTEM

Air conditioning is not simply the cooling of air. Air conditioning involves many aspects of conditioning or changing the air in whatever way in order to make the living environment of a building comfortable for the occupants. This conditioning may include warming the air, cooling the air, adding moisture, dehumidifying the air, filtering the air, and maintaining a balanced distribution or circulation of the air.

Air conditioning includes:

- heating;
- cooling;
- humidification;
- dehumidification;
- cleaning and filtering;
- air movement and circulation; and
- humidity.

Humidity refers to the water vapor or moisture content in the air. Water vapor is actually steam at low temperatures and low pressures. Air can carry water vapor, depending on its temperature. When air absorbs moisture (when it is humidified), the latent heat of evaporation must be supplied from the air or by some other means.

When moisture from the air is condensed, the latent heat of condensation is recovered. Air is referred to as saturated when it is carrying the maximum water vapor that it can hold.

## Humidification

Humidification is the addition of moisture to the air. A humidifier is a device that adds moisture to the air.

## Dehumidification

Dehumidification is the removal of moisture from the air. A dehumidifier is a device that removes moisture from the air. Dehumidifying is accomplished by condensation, which takes place when the temperature of the air is lowered below its dew point.

## The Dew Point

The dew point is the temperature of saturation at a certain atmospheric pressure. For a given atmospheric pressure, the dew point is the temperature at which moisture condenses into water droplets or dew. A reduction in temperature below the dew point will cause condensation of some of the water vapor. With the formation of condensate, there will be a release of some latent heat of the vapor, which will have to be absorbed and taken away before any more condensation can form.

## Compression and Cooling

Compression can be used to cool the air that is being conditioned. The refrigerant gas in the air conditioner coils is being compressed. When the gas expands and contracts, cool temperatures are produced. Simply put, when you increase pressure on a gas, the temperature increases.

## Rule of Thumb for Sizing Air Conditioners

The problem with using a "rule of thumb" is that it is inherently imprecise. The idea is to estimate the size of an air-conditioning unit. The rule is 1 ton of refrigeration for each 500 to 700 square feet of floor area in the building. A ton of refrigeration is equivalent to 12,000 BTU per hour.

Determining the size of an air-conditioner system can be difficult. It can be done by reading the model number on the data plate of the outdoor condenser unit. The Carrier Blue Book is a great resource that has model numbers, serial numbers, and efficiency ratings.

The size can be approximated by looking at the RLA (rated load amperage) number.

A compressor may be rated at 6 to 8 amps per ton of cooling. Modern compressors may draw about 5 amps. Take the RLA amp number and divide it by 6 to 8 (or 5, if the compressor is a newer model). That result is a good guess of the proper tonnage.

The size can be approximated by looking at the model number, finding the middle number, and dividing it by 12. The result is the tonnage.

Be careful when guessing the size of the air conditioner. You will probably be wrong.

## Cooling Methods

There are several ways to supply cool air to a building. Air conditioning can be achieved by the following methods:

- evaporative cooling;
- cold-water cooling;
- gas-compression refrigeration;
- gas-absorption refrigeration;
- thermo-electric refrigeration; and
- cooling with steam.

*Heat Pump*

The most common type of air-conditioning system in most homes is referred to as a direct-expansion, mechanical gas-compression (or vapor-compression) refrigeration system. This system consists of an indoor coil (evaporator coil), outdoor coil (condenser), and a pump (compressor).

A typical type of air-conditioning system installation is a split system whose compressor and air-cooled condenser unit are located outside, and the evaporator coil, fan and heating system are located inside the building. The evaporator and condenser coils are typically made of copper tubing with aluminum fins.

## Split System Air Conditioning

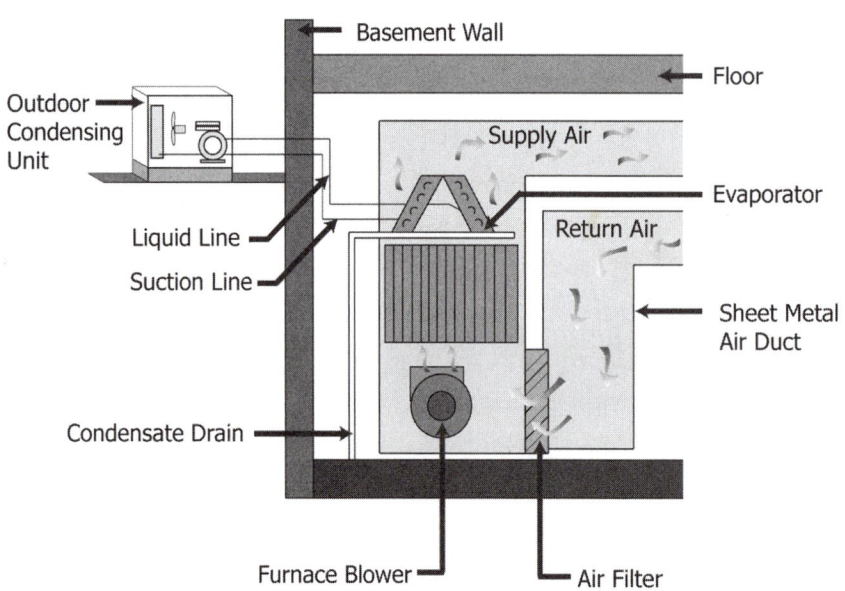

## Evaporative Cooling

An evaporative cooler (or swamp cooler) cools the indoor air using evaporation. It lowers the dry-bulb temperature of the indoor air.

The major components of an evaporative cooler are the:

- cabinet;
- water pump;
- blower and motor;
- media or water pads; and
- pump.

When the blower fan turns on, it draws air from outside. The air passes over the wet pads and blows into the interior. The water in the pads absorbs the heat from the air as it passes through them. This causes some evaporation of the water, and the temperature of the air is lowered. It is this creation of a low dry-bulb temperature that produces the cooling effect.

Evaporative coolers should not be installed where there is high humidity. They are used in dry climates. They are often mounted on top of a roof, but they can be inserted in a window opening or sidewall of a building, as well. Maintenance involves keeping the unit clean by cleaning or replacing the water pads, and cleaning the water sump tray and fan.

## Gas-Compression Cooling

Gas-compression cooling involves the compression and expansion of refrigerant gas and the transfer of heat. Heat is removed from the interior air and is released outside. Heat is simply transferred from one place to another.

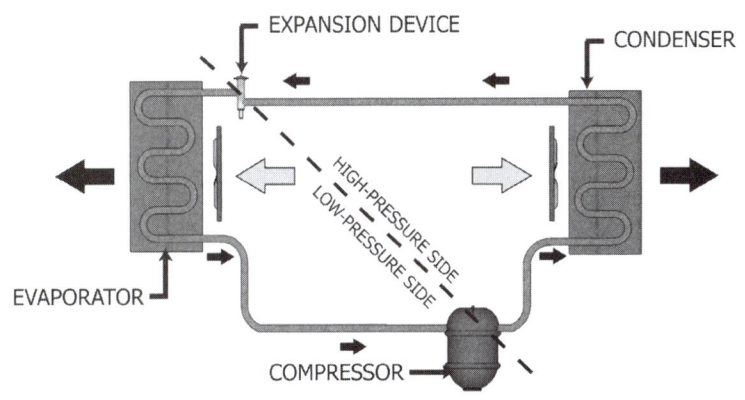

REFRIGERATION CYCLE

A gas-compression cooling system consists of the following components:

- the compressor;
- the condenser coil;
- the expansion device;
- the evaporator coil; and
- fans.

The compressor acts as a pump and pushes the liquid refrigerant through the liquid line to the expansion device. The liquid refrigerant is under high pressure in the liquid line. The expansion device is located at the evaporator coil.

The expansion device controls the flow of refrigerant into the evaporator coil. The device can be an expansion valve or a capillary tube.

As the high-pressure liquid refrigerant is forced through the expansion device, it expands into a larger volume in the evaporator coil. When it expands, its pressure is reduced and its boiling temperature is lowered. Under this low pressure, the liquid refrigerant boils until it becomes a vapor. During this change of state, the refrigerant absorbs heat from the warm indoor air flowing across the evaporator coil.

After the refrigerant has boiled or vaporized, the vapor moves out of the coil to the outdoor condenser unit through the suction line and enters the compressor. The compressor compresses the refrigerant vapor, increasing its temperature and pressure. The compressor pushes the vapor along the condenser.

At the condenser, the hot vapor is cooled. It is cooled by the outdoor air being blown through the coils of the condenser. When the air passes through the coils, it absorbs some of the refrigerant heat. The heat is transferred from the refrigerant in the coil to the air passing through.

The temperature of the air blowing out of the condenser increases, and the temperature of the refrigerant vapor decreases until the vapor is cooled to its saturation point. At that point, the vapor condenses into a liquid.

This refrigerant liquid is still under high pressure. It is pushed to the expansion device (valve or tube), and the cycle continues.

Cold is never created in this type of air-conditioning system. Instead, heat is transferred from one place to another. Heat is absorbed from the interior air, moved outside and released to the outdoor air. When heat is absorbed from the interior air, the air temperature is cooled.

## Air Temperature Drop

When an air conditioner is running, the house air may have a temperature drop of around 14° to 22° as the air moves across the evaporator coil. If you measure the temperature in the return duct at 80° F, the air temperature in the supply plenum would be around 58° F to 66° F. You may sense the temperature drop with your hand placed on the duct.

## Efficiency Ratings

The efficiency of cooling systems in a residential installation is expressed in terms of its seasonal energy efficiency ratio, or SEER. New air conditioners manufactured today must have a SEER rating of 13 or higher.

In January 2006, a U.S. government mandate required that manufacturers of heat pumps and air-conditioning systems could no longer make equipment with a SEER of less than 13. This 30% increase in minimum efficiency (from 10 SEER to 13 SEER) could result in energy savings of up to 23% compared to most central air-conditioning systems rated at 10 SEER.

If the air-conditioner system that you inspect is at least 10 years old, it could have a SEER rating as low as 8. However, homeowners are not required to replace their existing unit if it is less than 13 SEER.

## Central Air-Conditioner and Heat-Pump Cooling Efficiency (SEER) Based on Year of Manufacture:

- 1970 and earlier: SEER = 6
- 1971 to 1996: SEER = 9.5
- 1997 to 2002: SEER = 10.75
- 2003 to 2007: SEER = 11.2
- 2008 and later: SEER = 13

## Heat-Pump Heating Efficiency (HSPF):

- 1970 and earlier: HSPF = 5
- 1971 to 2007: HSPF = 5.5
- 2008 and later: HSPF = 7.7

### Room (Window) Air-Conditioner Cooling Efficiency (EER):

- 1972 and earlier: EER = 6
- 1973 to 1994: EER = 6
- 1995 to 1998: EER = 9
- 1999 to 2001: EER = 9
- 2002 and later: EER = 9.75

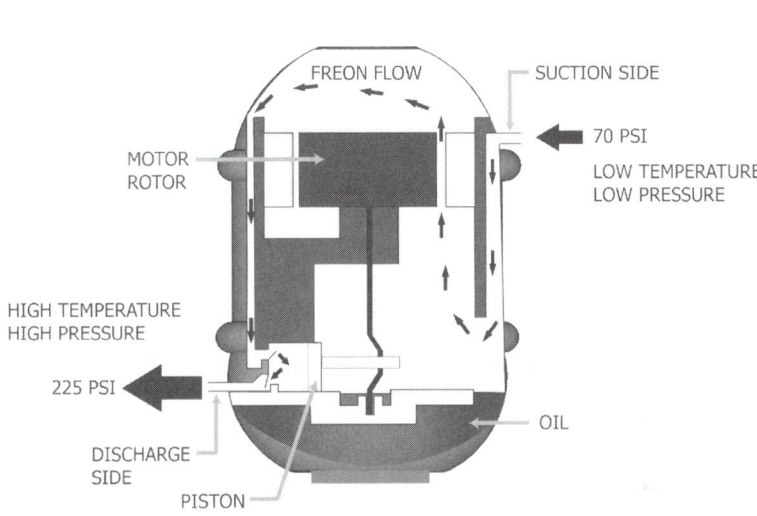

### Compressor

A compressor is a pump. It is located inside the outdoor condenser unit. It receives the low-pressure refrigerant vapor through the suction line and compresses or squeezes it into a smaller volume at a higher pressure. The compressor makes the pressure difference in the system, and it pushes or forces the refrigerant to flow around the system.

There are different types of compressors. They include reciprocating or piston, scroll, rotary, centrifugal, and screw-type. The scroll compressor is a relatively new design.

### Inspection Restrictions

Compressors should not be operated when it's below 65° F outside. Compressors should not be operated when the electricity has been turned on for less than 24 hours. Under these conditions, it is possible to damage the compressor. Oil may be mixed with the refrigerant in the base of the compressor.

### Compressor Heater

Many air-conditioning systems have a heater (a sump heater or crankcase heater) installed on the bottom of the compressor. The heater keeps the oil at the base of the compressor warm enough to boil off the refrigerant. The heater may be internal and not visible, or it may be visible on the outside as a ring wrapped around the compressor base. If the electricity has been turned off to the system, it may take 12 to 24 hours for the heater to warm up the oil sufficiently to boil off the refrigerant.

### Condenser

In a typical air-conditioning split system, the condenser unit (or outdoor coil) is located outside. A condenser condenses or liquefies the gas by cooling it. When the condenser is running, hot refrigerant gas coming from the compressor enters the condenser coil at the top. As it passes down through the condenser coil, it cools. The compressor is located inside the condenser unit.

The condenser can be a plain tube design, finned tube, or plate-type. It can be a series-pass or parallel-pass type. Condenser units can be air-cooled (the most common for residential installations), water-cooled, or a combination of the two.

An air-cooled condenser is made up of a coil that air blows across to cool the hot gas that's passing through the coil. There is a fan inside the condenser that pushes the air through the coil. Heat is transferred from the hot gases that are moving in the coil to the air passing through the coil.

If you put your hand in the path of the air blowing out of an operating condenser, it should feel warm.

Air-cooled condensers must be maintained and kept clean and free of debris and damage. The fins on the condenser coils can be easily damaged and bent. Damaged and bent fins can block the air flow through the condenser coil. A fin comb is an implement that can be used to straighten the fins back to their original position.

## Evaporator

An evaporator is sometimes called an evaporator coil, cooling coil, or indoor blower coil. In a typical residential air-conditioning system, the evaporator absorbs the heat energy from the air passing through it. It transfers the heat energy from the passing air to the refrigerant moving inside it. As the liquid refrigerant absorbs the heat, it is boiled off or evaporated as it moves through the evaporator. The house's air temperature drops as it passes through the coil, pushed by the blower fan.

Evaporators are usually made of copper tubing with closely spaced aluminum fins. There are about 14 aluminum fins per inch of copper tubing. This type of finned coil provides a very good surface area for transferring heat. Some coils are made of aluminum tubing, which does not last as long as copper tubing.

The evaporator coil is sometimes called an A-coil because some are shaped like the letter A. Some coils are called slab coils because they appear like a slab tilted at an angle. Coils have a condensate tray underneath to catch the condensate water draining off the coil.

Similar to the condenser, the evaporator coil must be maintained and kept clean and free of dirt, dust and damage.

## Refrigerant

Refrigerant is a substance that absorbs heat as it expands or vaporizes. A good refrigerant has a low boiling point and functions with a positive pressure.

### Expansion Device for Refrigerant Line

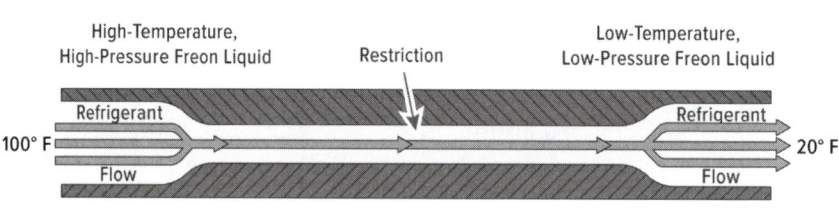

Metering/Expansion Device

The two most commonly used refrigerants in older air-conditioning systems are R-12 (Freon® 12) and R-22 (Freon® 22). R-12 has a boiling point of -21.8° F at atmospheric pressure. R-22 has a boiling point of -41.4° F.

R-410A is replacing those older refrigerants because it does not deplete ozone. R-410A can be recognized by its various trade names, including Genetron® AZ-20®, DuPont™ Suva®, and Puron®.

## Expansion Device

An expansion device changes the refrigerant from a high-pressure, high-temperature liquid to a low-pressure, low-temperature liquid. It is installed just before the evaporator.

There are two common expansion devices:

- capillary tubes; and
- thermostatic expansion valves.

The expansion device controls the flow of liquid refrigerant that enters the evaporator coil. If the valve is faulty, the flow of refrigerant may be restricted. The proper operation of the valve is largely dependent on the proper installation of the sensor bulb (or feeler bulb). The bulb needs to be in firm contact with the line of the evaporator.

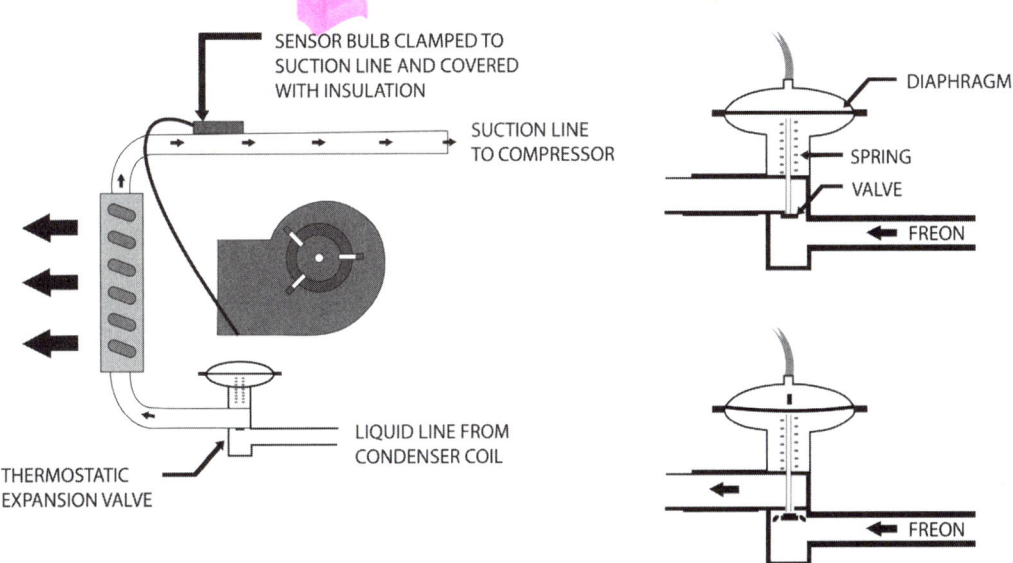

THERMOSTATIC EXPANSION VALVE

## Capillary Tube

The capillary tube is a coil of small-diameter copper tubing. It's designed to create a restriction or bottleneck in the liquid line. The refrigerant comes out of the small-diameter tube and expands as it enters a larger-diameter tube. This expansion lowers the pressure and temperature.

## Valve

A thermostatic expansion valve is another expansion device. It's a more precise device than the capillary tube. It controls the flow of refrigerant by sensing the heat that's coming out of the evaporator coil. A sensing bulb is mounted on the outlet pipe downstream of the coil.

## Refrigerant Piping

The air-conditioning system has refrigerant traveling through small-diameter copper pipes or tubing called refrigerant lines.

The suction line is the pipe going from the evaporator coil (inside the house) to the compressor (inside the condenser unit). The suction line carries the vapor (not liquid).

The liquid line is the pipe going from the condenser coil (in the condenser unit) to the evaporator. The liquid line carries the liquid (not the vapor).

All lines should be checked for damage and bent sections. A squeezed or pinched line will restrict proper flow.

The suction and liquid lines should not touch or come in contact with one another. The warm liquid line would then transfer heat to the cooler suction line.

If the evaporator (indoor unit) is installed higher in elevation than the condenser (outdoor unit), there should ideally be a slope to the suction line with a fall of ¼-inch per linear foot toward the condenser (outdoor unit).

## Filter Dryer

A filter removes particles from the liquid refrigerant and from the oil. A dryer (drier or dehydrator) removes moisture from the refrigerant. The filter-dryer device is a combination of the two. It is usually installed in the liquid line.

## Electrical Disconnect

According to modern standards, air-conditioning condensing units and heat pump units should have a readily accessible electrical disconnect within sight of the unit as the only allowable means. The disconnect is allowed to be installed on or within the unit, but it should not be located on panels designed to allow access to the unit. (Refer to NEC 440.14, Location of Electrical Disconnecting Means.)

# Quiz #8

1. T/F: Gas-compression cooling involves the compression and expansion of refrigerant gas and the transfer of heat.

   ☑ True
   ☐ False

2. The efficiency of a residential cooling system is expressed in terms of its ____.

   ☐ UFAE
   ☐ SEAR
   ☑ SEER

3. The _____ is located inside the outdoor condenser unit and receives the low-pressure refrigerant vapor through the suction line, and compresses or squeezes it into a smaller volume at a higher pressure.

   ☐ condenser
   ☑ compressor
   ☐ evaporator

4. In a typical residential air-conditioning system, the _____ absorbs the heat energy from the air passing through it, and transfers the heat energy from the passing air to the refrigerant moving inside it.

   ☐ capillary tube
   ☐ condenser
   ☑ evaporator

5. According to modern standards, air-conditioning condensing units and heat pump units should have a readily accessible electrical disconnect within ____ of the unit.

   ☐ 50 feet
   ☑ sight
   ☐ 1 foot

**Answer Key is on page 118.**

# Heat Pumps

## Introduction

Standard air-source heat pumps, ground-source heat pumps, and ductless mini-split heat pumps all provide cooling as well as heating. Heat pumps also dehumidify like air conditioners.

## Air-Source Heat Pump Heating Cycle

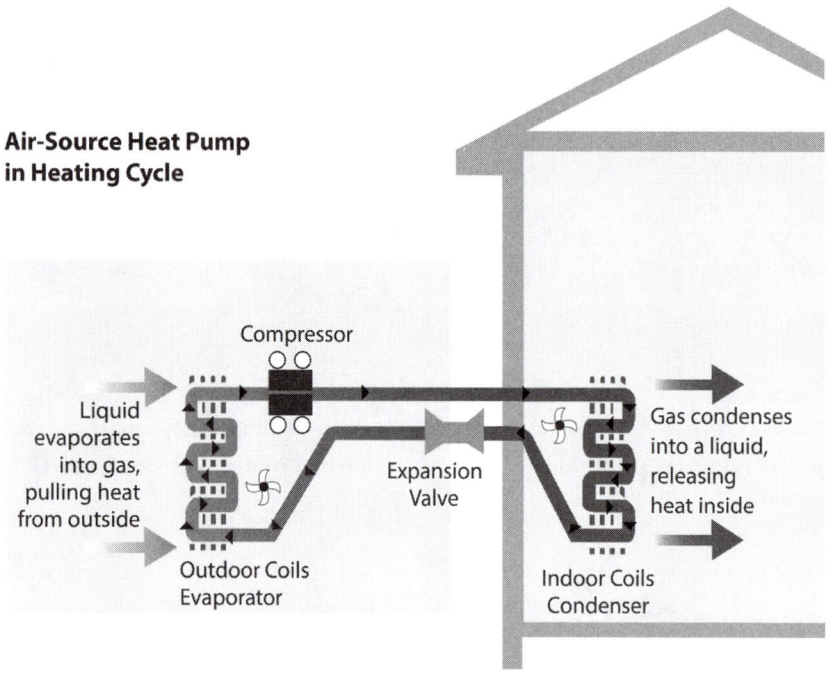

**Air-Source Heat Pump in Heating Cycle**

In heating mode, an air-source heat pump evaporates a refrigerant in the outdoor coil. As the liquid evaporates, it pulls heat from the outside air. The hot gas is compressed and pressurized as it passes through the compressor to the indoor coil (or condenser). Here it condenses to a high-pressure liquid, releasing heat to the inside of the house as it cools. The liquid then passes outside and through a pressure-lowering expansion valve and enters another heat exchanger (the evaporator), where the fluid absorbs heat and boils. The pressure changes caused by the compressor and the expansion valve allow the gas to evaporate at a low temperature outside and condense at a higher temperature indoors. In cooling mode, the reverse happens.

## Air-Source Heat Pump Cooling Cycle

In cooling mode, an air-source heat pump evaporates a refrigerant in the indoor coil. As the liquid evaporates, it pulls heat from the air in the house. After the gas is compressed, it passes into the outdoor coil and condenses, releasing heat to the outside air. The pressure changes caused by the compressor and the expansion valve allow the gas to condense at a high temperature outside and evaporate at a lower temperature indoors.

## Heat Pumps

A heat pump transfers heat from one place to another. It takes heat from the outdoor air and brings it to the inside of a building and releases it. With the use of a reversing valve, the heat pump can also take heat from the indoor air and release it outside. During the "reversed" cycle, the heat pump operates just like an air-conditioning system. Both the indoor coil and outdoor coil may act as either an evaporator or a condenser.

## Types of Heat Pumps

There are three types of heat pumps used in residential and light commercial installations. They are:

- air-source heat pumps;
- ground-source heat pumps; and
- water-source heat pumps.

Most heat pumps used in residential and light commercial installations are split-system heat pumps. A split-system heat pump is one that has its components divided, with the condenser unit (which holds the compressor) installed outside the building, and the evaporator coil (with the expansion device) located inside the building.

## Air-Source Heat Pumps

An air-source heat pump is often called an air-to-air heat pump, which uses the outdoor air as the source for heat. It uses the outdoor air as the source from which to absorb heat energy. It takes that heat energy from the outdoor air and transfers it to the interior air of the building.

The problem with air-source heat pumps occurs when the heat pump is operating in the cold wintertime and there's very little heat energy in the outdoor air due to low outdoor temperatures. And that is the same time that you want the heat pump to produce the most heat. For this reason, a supplementary radiant heating element is integrated into the system to be used during those conditions of very cold outdoor temperatures. Air-source heat pumps work well in areas where the winter temperature does not drop below 30° F for extended periods of time.

## Ground-Source Heat Pump

A ground-source heat pump is sometimes called a geothermal heat pump. A ground-source heat pump uses the constant temperature of the earth instead of the outdoor air as the heat source or heat sink, depending on the cycle.

A heat-transfer fluid is pushed through a bunch of underground, high-strength plastic pipes. The pipes are often coiled and looped or zigzagged. Horizontal loops are common in residential installations. There are horizontal closed-loop, spiral closed-loop, and vertical closed-loop systems.

Ground-source heat pumps are identified by many other names, including:

- water-source heat pumps;
- well-water heat pumps;
- direct-expansion heat pumps;
- geothermal heat pumps;
- groundwater heat pumps;
- earth-coupled heat pumps;
- ground-coupled heat pumps; and
- open-loop heat pumps.

## Water-Source Heat Pump

A water-source heat pump uses water as the heat source (or heat sink). Water is the heat-transfer medium. The constant temperature of the water source is used instead of the variable air temperature. The compressor and controls of a water-source heat pump are identical to those in a ground-source heat pump.

## Three Cycles

There are three cycles for a heat pump:

- the heating cycle;
- cooling cycle; and
- defrost cycle.

## Heating Cycle

In the heating cycle, the refrigerant enters the outdoor coil or condenser unit and moves through the outdoor coil. Inside the coil, the refrigerant starts out as a liquid in a low-pressure, low-temperature liquid state. The liquid absorbs heat energy from the outdoor air passing through the coil. The temperature of the liquid is raised up to its boiling point. The refrigerant boils into a hot vapor in the coil. The compressor then compresses the gas. The vapor pressure is increased. The high-pressure, high-temperature vapor is pushed through the suction line and into the evaporator coil (indoor unit). Heat is transferred or released to the indoor air (which is much cooler than the hot vapor), passing through the evaporator (indoor) coil. The cooler air passing through the indoor coil causes the gas to cool and condense into a liquid, which is still under high pressure.

The condensing of the high-pressure, high-temperature refrigerant vapor releases heat energy to the interior air of the building. The liquid then goes through a pressure-reducing valve or expansion valve and becomes a low-temperature, low-pressure liquid. This liquid is now in the liquid line and travels to the outdoor coil or condenser unit, where the cycle begins again.

The reversing valve allows the refrigerant to flow in the opposite direction. The compressor pumps the refrigerant in a cycle that can be reversed. The indoor coil and the outdoor coil change their functions based on the cycle called for.

## Cooling Cycle

In the cooling cycle, the valve is reversed, and the compressor pumps the refrigerant in the direction that results in the heat pump system absorbing heat energy from the interior air and releasing it outside. The heat pump system operates just like a regular air-conditioning system.

At the condenser, the hot refrigerant vapor (vapor with a lot of heat energy) is cooled by the outdoor air being blown through the coils of the condenser. When the air passes through the coils, it absorbs some of the refrigerant heat. As the passing air absorbs heat, the vapor in the coil gives off heat. The heat is transferred from the refrigerant in the coil to the air passing through. Heat that was absorbed from the indoor air is released outside.

## Defrost Cycle

When a heat pump is operating in the heating mode or heat cycle, the outdoor air is relatively cool and the outdoor coil acts as an evaporator. Under certain conditions of temperature and relative humidity, frost may form on the surface of the outdoor coil. This layer of frost will interfere with the operation of the heat pump by making the pump work harder and, therefore, inefficiently. The frost must be removed. A heat pump has a cycle called a defrost cycle, which automatically removes the frost from the outdoor coil.

A heat pump unit will defrost regularly when frost conditions occur. The defrost cycle should be long enough to melt the ice, and short enough to be energy-efficient.

In the defrost cycle, the heat pump is automatically operated in reverse for a moment in the cooling cycle. This action temporarily warms up the outdoor coil and melts the frost from the coil. In this defrost cycle, the outdoor fan is prevented from turning on when the heat pump switches over, and the temperature rise of the outdoor coil is accelerated and increased.

The heat pump will operate in the defrost cycle until the outdoor coil temperature reaches around 57° F. The time it takes to melt and remove accumulated frost from an outdoor coil varies, depending on the amount of frost and the internal timing device of the system.

## Interior Heating Element

During the defrost cycle of an older heat pump, the indoor unit may be operating with the fan blowing cool air. To prevent cool air from being produced and distributed inside the house, an electric heating element can be installed and engaged at the same time as the defrost cycle. In defrost mode, this heating element will automatically turn on, or the interior blower fan will turn off. The heating component is wired up to the second stage of a two-stage thermostat.

## Compressor

The compressor gets the refrigerant vapor at low pressure and compresses or squeezes it into a high-pressure, high-temperature vapor. Then the compressor pushes the vapor to one of the coils, depending on the heating or cooling cycle.

## The Typical Defrost Cycle

The components that make up the defrost cycle system include a thermostat, a timer, and a relay. There is a special thermostat or sensor of the defrost cycle system, often referred to as the frost thermostat. It is located on the bottom of the outdoor coil where it can detect the temperature of the coil.

When the outdoor coil temperature drops to around 32° F, the thermostat closes the circuit and makes the system respond. This causes an internal timer to start. Many heat pumps have a generic timer that energizes the defrost relays at certain timed intervals. Some generic timers will energize the defrost cycle every 30, 60 and 90 minutes.

The defrost relays turn on the compressor, switch the reversing valve of the heat pump, turn on the interior electric heating element, and stop the fan at the outdoor coil from spinning. The unit is now in the defrost cycle.

The unit remains in the defrost cycle (or cooling cycle) until the thermostat on the bottom of the outdoor coil senses that the outdoor coil temperature has reached about 57° F. At that temperature, the outdoor coil should be free of frost. The frost thermostat opens the circuit, stops the timer, and then the defrost cycle stops. The internal heater turns off, the valve reverses, and the unit returns to the heating cycle. A typical defrost cycle may run from 30 seconds to a few minutes. The defrost cycle should repeat regularly at timed intervals. The inspector should not observe a rapid cycling of the defrost operation.

In summary, certain conditions can force a heat pump into a defrost cycle (or cooling cycle) when the fan in the outdoor coil is stopped, the indoor fan is stopped or electric heat is turned on, and the frost melts and is removed from the outdoor coils. When the frost thermostat is satisfied (or a certain pre-set time period elapses), the outdoor fan comes back on, and the heat pump goes back into the heating cycle.

One problem of many older heat-pump systems is that the unit will operate in the defrost cycle regardless of whether ice is present. On these systems, if it's cold outside, the defrost cycle may turn on when it's not needed.

If the defrost cycle is not working properly, the outdoor coil will appear like a big block of ice and the unit won't function. Damage could result if the heat pump operates without a functional, normally operating defrost cycle.

## Causes of Frost

There are many reasons why an inspector may find frost and ice stuck on an outdoor coil of a heat pump that is not properly defrosting.

The cause of the frost and ice problem may include:

- a bad reversing valve;
- a damaged outdoor coil;
- a wiring problem;
- a bad thermostat;
- a leak in the refrigerant;
- a dirty outdoor coil covered with grass, dirt, debris and/or pet hair;
- a fan that won't turn on;
- a fan installed backwards, with the blades turning in the wrong direction;
- a motor operating in the incorrect direction; or
- a replacement fan motor spinning at a very low rpm.

Diagnosing apparent problems with the defrost cycle of a heat pump is beyond the scope of a home inspection, but such conditions should be deferred to a technician for further evaluation and servicing or repair.

# Air Cleaners and Filters

Home heating, ventilation, and air-conditioning (HVAC) systems that have a central air handler and ducting should be equipped with air filters. The purpose of air filters is to remove particulates (such as dust) from the air stream to protect the system from degradation by keeping internal components clean of particulate build-up that could cause lower equipment efficiency, reduced reliability, and diminished heat transfer.

HVAC filters are typically located in the return duct line adjacent to the air handler or on the back of the return register grille(s), where they trap particulates in the air pulled into the return ducts by the air handler. Filters are available in a range of styles, materials, and sizes. They're generally 1 to 4 inches thick, made of polyester and/or fiberglass, and styled in a flat or pleated pattern. Filters use either mechanical filtration or electrostatic filtration to remove particulates from the air. Mechanical (i.e., surface media) filtration is the capturing of particulates through a dense fiber medium.

The filter media are typically pleated, which allows more surface area to capture debris. Electrostatic filtration uses electrostatic precipitation to remove particulates. Some filter models on the market combine mechanical and electrostatic filtration. Filters can be replaceable, or washable and reusable. Replacement filters are typically made of synthetic media or fiberglass. They should be replaced every three months or sooner, if needed, especially if the HVAC equipment is used continuously. Filters loaded with particulates should be discarded. Washable filters typically use electrostatic filtration and are made of aluminum mesh or foam rubber. They should be removed for cleaning once every one to three months, rinsed with water or cleaning solution, air dried, and then re-installed. If washable air filters are not dried properly, they have the potential to attract mold.

Whole-house air filters come in four main types: flat filters, electronic filters, ultraviolet filters, and extended media filters.

## Flat Filters

If there is a forced-air furnace installed in the house, the HVAC system likely has a rudimentary air-filtration system, which is a thin plastic filter provided by the unit's manufacturer to capture very large particles. There are also matted-fiberglass filters that homeowners install. They should be changed once a month. When they clog, they stop working. And a clogged filter can damage the system over time because of the air restriction.

## Electronic Air Cleaners

Electronic air filters remove airborne particles from the air electronically, and they are more effective than conventional, disposable air filters. High-efficiency filters can remove about 80 to 90% of all particles.

Some electronic filters have a charged media pad or mat that is made of fiberglass, cellulose, or some similar material. When these pads get clogged or dirty, they usually cannot be washed and require replacement.

Some electronic air filters are two-stage filters. Air particles pass through not just one filtering device, but two electrically charged filters. There is typically a permanent screen or pre-filtering device. This first filter catches the larger particles before moving to the first electronic filter. In the first filter, the particles receive an intense positive charge. The positively charged particles are then attracted to the next filter that has collector plates. These plates are alternately charged with positive and negative voltages. The particles adhere to the negatively charged plates until the filter is removed and washed.

Most devices have a built-in performance-indicator light that glows red when the unit is operating normally. Many electronic air filters have a pre-filter (or lint filter) and an after-filter. The after-filter is installed after the second set of charged collector plates. Electronic air filters need to be cleaned at least once every six months. Most electronic air filters can be washed in the dishwasher, but the manufacturer's recommendations should be followed. When the filters are put back into place, they must be re-inserted correctly so that the air flows in the proper direction. There are usually directional arrows marked on the filter components to guide their proper installation.

ELECTRONIC AIR CLEANER

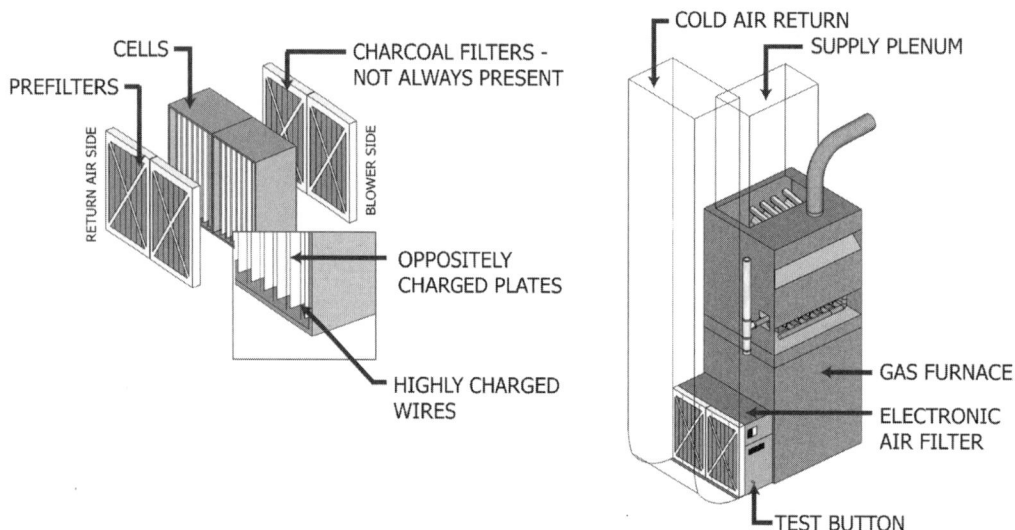

## Ultraviolet Filters

People worried primarily about germs may consider an ultraviolet filter. The ultraviolet light zaps airborne bacteria and viruses into oblivion, which is why hospitals use UV air filters in tuberculosis wards.

## Extended Media Filters

These filters are several inches thick and require a professional to install into the ductwork.

## HVAC Filter Performance and MERV

There are two elements of HVAC filter performance:

    1. the effectiveness at removing particles from the air; and

    2. resistance to airflow (i.e., pressure drop) across the filter.

The Minimum Efficiency Reporting Value (MERV) rating is one measure of a filter's ability to capture particles sized from 0.3 to 10 micrometers (μm) from the air stream. MERV rating corresponds to a level of performance ranging from 1 to 16; the higher the MERV rating, the more effective the filter is at capturing particles passing through it.

Another measure of a filter's effectiveness at removing particles is particle size efficiency, which is the fraction (or percentage) of particles captured on a filter. Particle size efficiency is measured across three particle size bins: 0.3 to 1.0 μm; 1.0 to 3.0 μm; and 3.0 to 10.0 μm. The percentages correspond to MERV ratings as shown in the table below, which is based on the National Air Filtration Association's Understanding MERV Guide, and the U.S. Environmental Protection Agency's (EPA) Residential Air Cleaners (Second Edition).

| MERV | Composite Average Particle Size Efficiency (%) in Size Range (μm) | | | Typical Applications | Typical Controlled Containment | Typical Filter Type |
|---|---|---|---|---|---|---|
| | Range 1: 0.3-1.0 μm | Range 2: 1.0-3.0 μm | Range 3: 3.0-10.0 μm | | | |
| 1 | n/a | n/a | $E_3 < 20\%$ | Minimal equipment protection in residential and light commercial applications | • Pollen<br>• Dust mites<br>• Spanish moss<br>• Carpet fibers<br>• Spray paint dust | • Permanent<br>• Self-charging<br>• Washable<br>• Metal<br>• Foam<br>• Disposable panels<br>• Fiberglass<br>• Synthetic |
| 2 | n/a | n/a | $E_3 < 20\%$ | | | |
| 3 | n/a | n/a | $E_3 < 20\%$ | | | |
| 4 | n/a | n/a | $E_3 < 20\%$ | | | |
| 5 | n/a | n/a | $20\% \le E_3 < 35\%$ | Good equipment protection in residential, minimal equipment protection in commercial and industrial applications | • Mold<br>• Spores<br>• Pet dander<br>• Hair spray<br>• Fabric protector<br>• Powdered milk | • Pleated filters<br>• Extended surface filters<br>• Media panel filters |
| 6 | n/a | n/a | $35\% \le E_3 < 50\%$ | | | |
| 7 | n/a | n/a | $50\% \le E_3 < 70\%$ | | | |
| 8 | n/a | n/a | $70\% \le E_3$ | | | |
| 9 | n/a | $E_2 < 50\%$ | $85\% \le E_3$ | Superior equipment protection in residential applications, good equipment protection in commercial and industrial applications | • Legionella<br>• Humidifier dust<br>• Milled flour<br>• Auto emission particles | • Non-supported<br>• Pocket filter<br>• Rigid box<br>• Rigid cell<br>• Cartridge v-cells |
| 10 | n/a | $50\% \le E_2 < 65\%$ | $85\% \le E_3$ | | | |
| 11 | n/a | $65\% \le E_2 < 80\%$ | $85\% \le E_3$ | | | |
| 12 | n/a | $80\% \le E_2$ | $90\% \le E_3$ | | | |
| 13 | $E_1 < 75\%$ | $90\% \le E_2$ | $90\% \le E_3$ | Health care and hospitals, superior equipment protection in commercial applications | • Bacteria<br>• Cooking oil<br>• Most smoke<br>• Face powder<br>• Paint pigments | • Rigid cell<br>• Cartridge rigid box<br>• Non-supported<br>• Bag<br>• Pocket filter<br>• V-cells |
| 14 | $75\% \le E_1 < 85\%$ | $90\% \le E_2$ | $90\% \le E_3$ | | | |
| 15 | $85\% \le E_1 < 95\%$ | $90\% \le E_2$ | $90\% \le E_3$ | | | |
| 16 | $95\% \le E_1$ | $95\% \le E_2$ | $95\% \le E_3$ | | | |

## Pressure Drop or Airflow Resistance

The second aspect of HVAC filter performance is pressure drop or resistance to airflow. As the air stream passes through the filter, it decreases its velocity due to the resistance of the filter. This resistance is measured in inches of water column (IWC, or in. w.c.) at either a specific face velocity or airflow rate.

The resistance to airflow of a brand new filter is called the "initial pressure drop," whereas the resistance when the filter is loaded with particulates is called the "final pressure drop." The contribution of the filter to the total system pressure drop is typically 20% to 50%, depending on the system's configuration, filter efficiency, and loading condition. HVAC system engineers and designers are supposed to take the initial pressure drop of the filter into account when determining how to size HVAC equipment and related ductwork for residential and commercial buildings.

## Resistance Causes Energy Consumption

The resistance to airflow in a high static pressure system causes the controls of brushless permanent magnet (BPM) blower motors to increase speed and power draw to maintain system airflow, resulting in an increase in energy consumption. Permanent split capacitor (PSC) blower motors do not have airflow controls like BPM blower motors and thus will not increase power and speed to maintain system airflow. Instead, since PSC blower motors cannot adjust speed or torque, they reduce power draw and airflow in response to increasing system pressures. This is known as "fall off," when the motor will stop pushing even though the fan continues to turn. As a result, the run time necessary to cool or heat the ambient air to the thermostat's set point temperature is extended, which can lead to an overall increase in energy use. In addition, excessive pressure drop can damage the furnace due to overheating, can freeze condensing coils in air conditioning units, and can burn out blower motors.

It's important for homeowners to purchase filters with a pressure drop performance that meets their HVAC system's specifications in order to run their equipment efficiently and prevent damage. The Air Conditioning Contractors of America (ACCA) Manual D Residential Duct Systems offers guidance for sizing residential ducting systems, including sizing HVAC filters for pressure drop in the system.

## High MERV Can Clog Faster

The accumulation of dirt and particles can greatly increase pressure drop across a filter. Because high-MERV filters can trap more particles, they are likely to clog faster than low-MERV filters. Choosing filters with deeper pleats (e.g., 4-inch pleats) will increase the surface area of the filter and potentially reduce the pressure drop while increasing or maintaining a high MERV rating. For example, a filter that has 4-inch-high pleats has twice the surface area of a filter with 2-inch-high pleats. If a homeowner wants to use a very high MERV filter, it may require the alteration or replacement of ducting if the pressure drop of the filter is greater than the pressure drop allotted to the filter in the system design. Another option is to advise the homeowner to purchase separate air filtration equipment that can clean the indoor air without impacting the performance of the HVAC equipment. Filters should be selected as part of the overall duct design process, as described in the Air Conditioning Contractors of America (ACCA) Manual D Residential Duct Systems.

## Accessible for Homeowners

Making filters accessible for easy replacement and providing controls that tell homeowners when replacement is due will help to eliminate problems, such as clogging and filter collapse, which are more likely to occur with higher MERV filters. If exceptionally high filtration is desired (above MERV 13), some sources suggest using separate air filtration equipment with a HEPA filter that can clean the air without impacting furnace performance, although their functionality is localized, as opposed to whole-house.

## How to Select a High MERV Filter

The builder or HVAC contractor should design the HVAC duct system using ACCA Manual D to determine the maximum static pressure that the filter can have and select a MERV 6 or higher filter within that limit, and adjust the duct size, duct length, and/or filter surface area as necessary to ensure that the total pressure drop across the system does not exceed the blower fan motor's limit, given the size of the unit.

## Recommend MERV 6 or Higher

In homes with ducted HVAC equipment, the HVAC inspector should look for HVAC systems with filters that are rated MERV 6 or higher. The HVAC technician or builder should have ensured that the HVAC system can accommodate the pressure drop associated with higher MERV filters. When certifying ENERGY STAR-certified homes, the HERS rater inspects to make sure that MERV 6 or higher filters are installed. When assessing EPA Indoor airPLUS and DOE Zero Energy Ready certified homes, the rater verifies that MERV 8 or higher filters are installed.

# Humidifiers

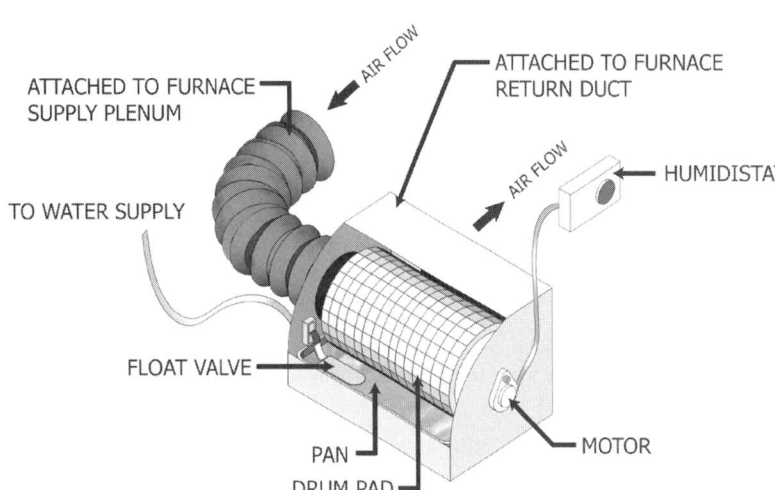

DRUM-TYPE HUMIDIFIER

ATTACHED TO FURNACE SUPPLY PLENUM

AIR FLOW

ATTACHED TO FURNACE RETURN DUCT

AIR FLOW

HUMIDISTAT

TO WATER SUPPLY

FLOAT VALVE

PAN

DRUM PAD

MOTOR

A humidifier adds moisture to the air primarily by evaporation, by the use of steam, or by spraying water particles.

A bypass humidifier is a common type. It contains an evaporator pad, drum, and wheel or belt. The pad gets wet and absorbs moisture. Warm air from the supply duct passes over the wet pad, causes the water to evaporate, and results in adding humidity to the air.

The operation of a humidifier is controlled by a humidistat that may be mounted on a wall in a room or on a furnace duct.

Many humidifiers use a bypass duct. The bypass duct goes between the supply duct and the return plenum. A damper should be installed in this bypass duct pipe. The damper is closed off when the humidifier is not in operation, typically during the summer months.

## Location

The common location for a bypass humidifier is on the underside of a horizontal warm-air supply duct, close to the furnace. Humidifiers are also installed on the sides of furnace plenums. The warm-air plenum is the most desirable location for a humidifier. The manufacturer's recommendations for installation must be followed.

## Maintenance

Moisture from humidifiers may support microbial growth on wet surfaces where it can condense during cold weather. Humidifiers that discharge small droplets of water from a reservoir are prone to support mold growth. Moisture accumulation inside dirty ductwork creates a suitable environment for mold growth. The reservoir of the humidifier usually becomes contaminated, to some degree. Humidifiers should be considered potential sources of mold growth.

All humidifiers use water, so delayed maintenance at a humidifier may cause indoor air quality issues for sensitive people. If there is a reservoir of water in the humidifier, then it needs to be drained and cleaned regularly. Humidifiers need regular maintenance, including cleaning, and the removal of lime and other residue. Any moisture pads or media need to be replaced regularly, usually every month while the humidifier is in regular operation.

## Levels

Indoor relative humidity (RH) should be between 20 and 40% in the winter, and less than 60% during the rest of the year. Some experts recommend that indoor humidity levels in general should be between 40 and 60%.

Understanding relative humidity in a building is essential to controlling mold growth. Relative humidity (RH) is a ratio, expressed as a percentage, of the amount of moisture in the air to the maximum amount of moisture that the air can hold. Warm air can hold more moisture than cool air. RH is a factor in determining how much moisture is present in a room, but it is the available moisture in a substrate, and not the RH of the room's air, that determines whether mold can grow.

Many sources recommend maintaining RH in living spaces below 60% to limit microbial growth. By keeping RH below 60%, one may assume that the moisture content of building materials would be low. However, this assumption may be false because mold grows on surfaces and in building materials, not in the air. Therefore, it is the RH in the air adjacent to the surface, and not the ambient RH, which must be lowered in order to control mold growth. Measuring a room with a relative humidity at or below 60% may mean that the building materials are fairly dry, but it does not eliminate the possibility of mold growth because local cold spots and water intrusion may allow the RH of the air adjacent to the surface to exceed 70%.

Moisture meters are essential tools for inspectors; they enable you to identify damp areas that would not be evident otherwise. Infrared cameras are praised for their ability to detect moisture that is not readily visible to the naked eye. Damp areas appear as cold spots, with gradient imaging appearing dark.

# Electric Furnaces

Electric furnaces produce heat almost instantly because there are no heat exchangers to warm up. The heating elements of an electric furnace start producing heat as soon as the thermostat calls for heat. There is no flame, no combustion, and no venting of gases to the outside. An electric furnace is 100% efficient. Electric furnaces can be upflow, downflow, or horizontal.

All heating systems require access for servicing and maintenance, including electric furnaces. A clearance of 24 to 30 inches should be provided in front of the heating system.

Electric furnaces need very little to no clearance between the furnace and combustibles but should still have 24 to 30 inches of open space in front for servicing and maintenance.

## Components

The components of an electric furnace include:

- automatic controls;
- heating elements;
- safety controls;
- a blower fan and motor; and
- air filtering.

## Thermostat

A thermostat controls the operation of the furnace. The thermostat senses the air temperature in the room or space that is being heated. When the thermostat calls for heat, it sends a signal to the first heating circuit. The heating circuit turns on, and there is usually a slight delay (15 seconds), and then the blower fan turns on. Another delay (30 seconds) happens before the second heating circuit turns on. All other heating circuits turn on in a similar fashion.

## Heating Elements

An electric heating element has to get very hot — hotter than its surroundings — in order to deliver the desired level of heat. It may get red-hot or nearly white-hot.

Wires with high heat resistance are used for heating elements. These include iron, chromium, nickel, manganese, and alloy wires.

## Controls and Components

Electric furnaces have a variety of safety controls installed in them. The controls protect the unit against overloading of electric current and from excessively high temperatures. The controls include:

- furnace fuses;
- temperature-limit controls;
- circuit breakers;
- transformers; and

• thermal-overload protectors.

One of the most important components of an electric furnace is the air filter. A clogged filter will cause the furnace to run inefficiently by making it run harder and longer. Air filters should be checked regularly — every month. Maintenance and repair should be conducted by a qualified technician because deadly high-voltage conditions exist within the electric heating system. The electrical supply should be turned off prior to servicing the unit.

# Conclusion

Now that you've finished this book, if you're an InterNACHI® member, be sure to take InterNACHI's online "How to Inspect HVAC Systems" course and final exam, which is a membership requirement. Once you have successfully completed them, you can download your Certificate of Completion. This accredited course is worth 12 Continuing Education credit hours.

After successful completion of the online course and exam, you should be able to perform an inspection of the HVAC system at a residential property, according to the InterNACHI® Standards of Practice for Performing a General Home Inspection.

Be sure to also take InterNACHI's "Advanced HVAC Training for Home Inspectors" video course that covers the steps of an HVAC inspection at

**www.nachi.org/advanced-training-inspecting-hvac-systems-online-video-course**

The HVAC Inspector logo is available for use by all InterNACHI® Certified members who successfully complete this book's related online course, including its final exam.

Download the logo from **www.nachi.org/logos**

# Appendix I: Answer Keys

## Answer Key for Quiz #1

1. T/F: A home inspection is a non-invasive, visual examination of a residential dwelling.
   Answer: **True**

2. T/F: A home inspector is required to describe the energy source.
   Answer: **True**

3. T/F: A home inspector is not required to describe the heating method.
   Answer: **False**

4. T/F: The inspector is required to inspect window and through-wall air-conditioning units.
   Answer: **False**

## Answer Key for Quiz #2

1. T/F: Heat moves from the warmer body, and the colder body absorbs it.
   Answer: **True**

2. Heat can move from one body to another by **radiation**.

3. Forced-air furnaces function primarily by **convection**.

## Answer Key for Quiz #3

1. T/F: You may be able to describe a heating system by its heat-conveying medium.
   Answer: **True**

2. T/F: Steam is considered a heat-conveying medium.
   Answer: **True**

3. Most heating systems can be categorized in **four** ways.

4. T/F: "Hydronic" describes a type of heating system.
   Answer: **True**

## Answer Key for Quiz #4

1. Burning natural gas with oxygen yields carbon dioxide, water vapor, and **heat**.

2. T/F: A natural draft unit has a draft fan.
   Answer: **False**

3. There are two broad categories that describe furnace heating systems: gravity warm-air furnaces; and **forced** warm-air furnaces.

4. A(n) **downflow** furnace is also referred to as a counterflow furnace or a down-draft furnace.

## Answer Key for Quiz #5

1. If you are inspecting a **plenum** duct system, you should find a large rectangular duct that comes directly out of the heating system and runs in a straight line down the center of the basement, attic or ceiling.

2. T/F: Round or square supply ducts that are connected to and branch off the extended duct are called side takeoffs.
   Answer: **True**

3. T/F: Diffusers are typically formed in concentric cones or pyramids.
   Answer: **True**

## Answer Key for Quiz #6

1. A **BTU** is approximately the amount of energy needed to heat 1 pound of water by 1° F.

2. Older gas furnaces have a(n) **standing** pilot light that is always burning.

3. T/F: There may be at least two heat exchangers inside a high-efficiency furnace.
   Answer: **True**

4. **Primary** air is air that mixes with the gas before going to the burners.

## Answer Key for Quiz #7

1. T/F: Air is the heat-conveying medium for hydronic heating systems.
   Answer: **False**

2. One cubic foot of water at 68° F weighs about **62** pounds.

3. T/F: Radiators and baseboard convectors are considered heat-emitting components.
   Answer: **True**

## Answer Key for Quiz #8

1. T/F: Gas-compression cooling involves the compression and expansion of refrigerant gas and the transfer of heat.
   Answer: **True**

2. The efficiency of a residential cooling system is expressed in terms of its **SEER**.

3. The **compressor** is located inside the outdoor condenser unit and receives the low-pressure refrigerant vapor through the suction line, and compresses or squeezes it into a smaller volume at a higher pressure.

4. In a typical residential air-conditioning system, the **evaporator** absorbs the heat energy from the air passing through it, and transfers the heat energy from the passing air to the refrigerant moving inside it.

5. According to modern standards, air-conditioning condensing units and heat pump units should have a readily accessible electrical disconnect within **sight** of the unit.

# EDUCATION & TRAINING BOOKS

Whether you're new to the business, an inspector seeking more information, or a veteran of the industry looking to expand your knowledge, these official InterNACHI® publications will help you become the best inspector you can be.

## We Offer the Following Education & Training Books:

- **How to Inspect the Exterior**
  Item Number: 0094

- **How to Perform Deck Inspections**
  Item Number: 0029

- **Residential Plumbing Overview**
  Item Number: 0064

- **Inspecting HVAC Systems**
  Item Number: 0061

- **Safe Practices for the Home Inspector**
  Item Number: 0038

- **Inspecting the Attic, Insulation, Ventilation & Interior**
  Item Number: 0109

- **How to Perform Electrical Inspections**
  Item Number: 0023

- **How to Inspect Pools & Spas**
  Item Number: 0076

- **How to Perform Roof Inspections**
  Item Number: 0042

- **How to Perform a Mold Inspection**
  Item Number: 0022

- **How to Perform Radon Inspections**
  Item Number: 0028

- **Inspecting Foundation Walls and Piers**
  Item Number: 0065

- **25 Standards Every Inspector Should Know**
  Item Number: 0037

- **How to Inspect for Moisture Intrusion**
  Item Number: 0073

- **International Standards of Practice for Inspecting Commercial Properties**
  Item Number: 0016

- **Structural Issues for Home Inspectors**
  Item Number: 0059

The purpose of these publications is to provide accurate and useful information for home inspectors in order to perform an inspection of the various systems at a residential property. They also serve as study aids for InterNACHI's online courses, as well as reference manuals for on the job.

**Find these books plus more tools to grow your inspection business at**
**www.InspectorOutlet.com**

# INSPECTOR OUTLET

## YOU'LL BE SHOCKED BY OUR LOW PRICES!

Inspector Outlet is your source for all things home inspection-related. We are the official store for InterNACHI® publications, equipment and apparel. We strive to provide the best products at the lowest prices in the industry.

InterNACHI® members get the best pricing on tools, testing equipment and meters.

Find an outstanding selection of original training manuals, checklists, articles and PDFs, as well as publications for clients, including the best-selling home maintenance guide, *Now That You've Had a Home Inspection*.

We offer a great line of protective outerwear and customized apparel for home inspectors, including shirts, jackets and hats.

InterNACHI's Inspector Marketing Department can design and print a variety of custom marketing materials for your home inspection business.

Protect yourself and your clients on the job with our specialized safety and inspection equipment that help make your inspections easier and safer.

Are you an InterNACHI® member? Inspector Outlet offers free inspector decals and embroidered patches to all eligible members!

## INSPECTOR OUTLET

**www.InspectorOutlet.com          Sales@InspectorOutlet.com**